COMPU[TER] MADE S[IMPLE]

C000319231

NEW
AOL 4.0
Keith Brindley
0 7506 4626 8 1999

NEW
Access 2000
Moira Stephen
0 7506 4182 7 1999

NEW
Access 2000 in Business
Moira Stephen 1999
7506 4611 X £11.99

Access 97 for Windows
Moira Stephen
0 7506 3800 1 1997

Access for Windows 95 (V.7)
Moira Stephen
0 7506 2818 9 1996

Access for Windows 3.1 (V.2)
Moira Stephen
0 7506 2309 8 1995

NEW
Adobe Acrobat & PDF
Graham Douglas
0 7506 4220 3 1999

NEW
Compuserve 2000
Keith Brindley
0 7506 4524 5 1999

Compuserve (V.3)
Keith Brindley
0 7506 3512 6 1998

NEW
Designing Internet Home Pages *Second Edition*
Lilian Hobbs
0 7506 4476 1 1999

Excel 2000
Stephen Morris
0 7506 4180 0 1999

NEW
Excel 2000 in Business
Stephen Morris 1999
0 7506 4609 8 £11.99

Excel 97 for Windows
Stephen Morris
0 7506 3802 8 1997

Excel for Windows 95 (V.7)
Stephen Morris
0 7506 2816 2 1996

Excel for Windows 3.1 (V.5)
Stephen Morris
0 7506 2070 6 1994

NEW
Explorer 5.0
P K McBride
0 7506 4627 6 1999

Explorer 4.0
Sam Kennington
0 7506 3796 X 1998

Explorer 3.0
Sam Kennington
0 7506 3513 4 1997

NEW
Internet In Colou[r]
P K McBride 1999
0 7506 4576 8 £14.99

NEW
Internet for Windows 98
P K McBride
0 7506 4563 6 1999

Internet for Windows 95
P K McBride
0 7506 3846 X 1997

NEW
FrontPage 2000
Nat McBride
0 7506 4598 9 1999

FrontPage 97
Nat McBride
0 7506 3941 5 1998

NEW
The iMac Made Simple
Keith Brindley
0 7506 4608 X 1999

NEW
Microsoft Money 99
Moira Stephen
0 7506 4305 6 1999

NEW
Publisher 2000
Moira Stephen
0 7506 4597 0 1999

Publisher 97
Moira Stephen
0 7506 3943 1 1998

MS-DOS
Ian Sinclair
0 7506 2069 2 1994

Multimedia for Windows 95
Simon Collin
0 7506 3397 2 1997

Netscape Communicator 4.0
Sam Kennington
0 7506 4040 5 1998

Netscape Navigator (V.3)
P K McBride
0 7506 3514 2 1997

NEW
Office 2000
P K McBride
0 7506 4179 7 1999

Office 97
P K McBride
0 7506 3798 6 1997

NEW
Outlook 2000
P K McBride
0 7506 4414 1 1999

NEW
Pagemaker (V.6.5)
Steve Heath
0 7506 4050 2 1999

NEW
Photoshop 5
Martin Evening
Rod Wynne-Powell
0 7506 4334 X 1999

Moira Stephen
0 7506 4177 0 1999

Powerpoint 97 for Windows
Moira Stephen
0 7506 3799 4 1997

Powerpoint for Windows 95 (V.7)
Moira Stephen
0 7506 2817 0 1996

NEW
Sage Accounts
P K McBride
0 7506 4413 3 1999

Searching the Internet
P K McBride
0 7506 3794 3 1998

Windows 98
P K McBride
0 7506 4039 1 1998

Windows 95
P K McBride
0 7506 2306 3 1995

Windows 3.1
P K McBride
0 7506 2072 2 1994

NEW
Windows CE
Craig Peacock
0 7506 4335 8 1999

Windows NT (V4.0)
Lilian Hobbs
0 7506 3511 8 1997

NEW
Word 2000
Keith Brindley
0 7506 4181 9 1999

NEW
Word 2000 in Business
Keith Brindley 1999
0 7506 4610 1 £11.99

Word 97 for Windows
Keith Brindley
0 7506 3801 X 1997

Word for Windows 95 (V.7)
Keith Brindley
0 7506 2815 4 1996

Word for Windows 3.1 (V.6)
Keith Brindley
0 7506 2071 4 1994

Word Pro (4.0) for Windows 3.1
Moira Stephen
0 7506 2626 7 1995

Works for Windows 95 (V.4)
P K McBride
0 7506 3396 4 1996

Works for Windows 3.1 (V.3)
P K McBride
0 7506 2065 X 1994

Includes New Titles for 1999

Access 2000
Made Simple

Moira Stephen

MADE SIMPLE
BOOKS

OXFORD AUCKLAND BOSTON JOHANNESBURG MELBOURNE NEW DELHI

Made Simple
An imprint of Butterworth-Heinemann
Linacre House, Jordan Hill, Oxford OX2 8DP
225 Wildwood Avenue, Woburn MA 01801-2041
A division of Reed Educational and Professional Publishing Ltd

⋐   A member of the Reed Elsevier plc group

First published 1999
© Moira Stephen, 1999

TRADEMARKS/REGISTERED TRADEMARKS
Computer hardware and software brand names mentioned in this book are protected
by their respective trademarks and are acknowledged.

British Library Cataloguing in Publication Data
A catalogue record for this book is available from the British Library

ISBN 0 7506 4182 7

Typeset by Elle and P.K.McBride, Southampton
Icons designed by Sarah Ward © 1994
Printed and bound in Great Britain

Contents

Preface

Welcome to *Access 2000 Made Simple*. This book is aimed at students, home users and owners of small business who will be setting up a basic database for their own use.

Using this book, you will learn how to:

- Get into Access and interrogate the on-line help system.
- Create a database and enter table structures.
- Enter and edit your data.
- Format the display of your data.
- Locate data in your tables by sorting and searching.
- Create a simple form to help make entering and editing data easier.
- Produce reports that present your data effectively.
- Build a database using a Wizard.

If you want to be able to harness the power of Access 2000 *without* being overpowered with database jargon and difficult concepts, then this book is for you. Whether you're new to databases, or are familiar with databases but new to Access 2000 – it doesn't matter – this book will have you up and running quickly and painlessly.

We know your time is precious, so the examples used throughout this book are kept simple so that you can learn to use the package in as little time as possible.

Take note

This book is also available in an extended business edition, with extra material on the use of forms, queries, reports and other Access features that allow you to get data into and information out of databases more effectively. If you are setting up databases for others to use, or need to output information for clients and colleagues, *Access 2000 Made Simple Business Edition* will show you how.

1 Getting Started

What is a database?

A **database** is simply a collection of data, stored in an organised fashion. For example, it may be an address list, employee details or details about items in stock.

Table

In database, all the data on one topic is stored in a **table**. You would have a table for your employee data, a table for your customer data, a table for your product data, etc. If your database requirements are fairly simple, you might have only one table in your database. If your requirements are more complex, your database may contain several tables.

The data in the table is structured in a way that will allow you to interrogate the data when and as required. All of the data on one item, e.g .an employee or a stock item, is held in the **record** for that employee or stock item, within the appropriate table.

Access is a **relational** database management sysytem. This means that an Access database can contain several tables of data which can be related to each other through common fields. This allows information to be stored very efficiently. For example, a retailer might have a table to hold the data on the goods that are stocked and a second table of suppliers, with the two linked through the suppliers' names. No matter how many different kinds of goods are bought from one supplier, it is only necessary to enter the full supplier details once (in the supplier table).

Record

A **record** contains information about a single item in your table. The details of one employee will be held in that employee's record; the detail on a customer will be held in a record for that customer. This information is broken down into several **fields**. Every record in the table will have the same structure of fields.

Tip

If you've never used a database package before, I suggest you read through the next few pages carefully. Database concepts and jargon are not difficult, but you need to appreciate how a database works and to become familiar with some of the jargon you will come across. If you're already familiar with databases, move on to 'Getting into Access' (page 8).

Field

A **field** is a piece of data within a record, identified by a name. In an employee's record things like forename, surname, job title, address, age, salary, etc. would all be held in separate fields. In a stock item record, you would have fields for stock number, description, price, etc. A database can be sorted or searched on the information held in a selected field, e.g. to pu the records into alphabetical order of surname, or find those records where the item is out of stock.

Company database file

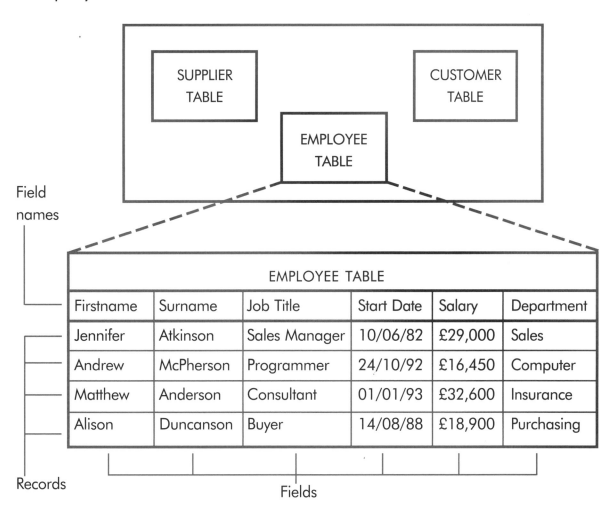

Field names

EMPLOYEE TABLE

Firstname	Surname	Job Title	Start Date	Salary	Department
Jennifer	Atkinson	Sales Manager	10/06/82	£29,000	Sales
Andrew	McPherson	Programmer	24/10/92	£16,450	Computer
Matthew	Anderson	Consultant	01/01/93	£32,600	Insurance
Alison	Duncanson	Buyer	14/08/88	£18,900	Purchasing

Records

Fields

Access objects

When working in Access, you find seven different types of **objects** that are used to input, display, interrogate, print and automate your work. These objects are listed on the tabs in the Database window.

Tables

Tables are the most important object in your database. Tables are used for data entry, viewing data and displaying the results of queries (see Chapters 3-8).

In a table, each record is displayed as a row and each field is displayed as a column. You can display a number of records on the screen at any one time, and as many fields as will fit on your screen. Any records or fields not displayed can be scrolled into view as required.

Queries

You use **queries** to locate specific records within your tables. You might want to extract records that meet specific selection criteria (e.g. all employees on Grade G in the accounts department). Calculations can also be performed on queries. When you run a query, the results are displayed in a table (see Chapter 8).

Forms

You can use **forms** to provide an alternative to tables for data entry and viewing records. With forms, you arrange the fields as required on the screen – you can design your forms to look like the printed forms (invoices, order forms, etc.) that you use.

When you use forms, you display one record at a time on your screen (see Chapter 9).

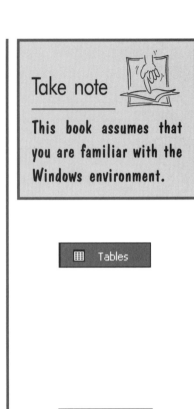

Take note

This book assumes that you are familiar with the Windows environment.

Reports

Reports can be used to produce various printed outputs from data in your database. Using reports, the same database can produce a list of customers in a certain area, a set of mailing labels for your letters, or a report on how much each customer owes you (see Chapter 10).

Pages

Data access pages are a special type of Web page. They are used for viewing and working with data stored in an Access database (or Microsoft SQL Server database) from the Internet or an intranet. Data access pages may include data from other sources, e.g. Excel. Pages are discussed in the Buisness Edition of this book.

Macros and modules

Macros and **modules** are used to automate the way you use Access, and can be used to build some very sophisticated applications. These are both are beyond the scope of this book, though macros are covered in the Business Edition.

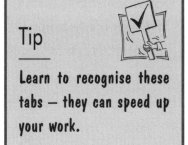

Take note

Access allows you to 'group' different objects that you use regularly into one place — in the Group Area. This allows you to access the objects you regularly use from one area.

A folder called Favorites is already set up for you in the Groups area. You can use this folder or set up your own. We'll discuss Groups in more detail later.

Preparing your data

The most important (and often difficult) stage in setting up your database takes place away from the computer. Before you set up a database you must get your data organised.

You must ask yourself two key questions:

●   What do I want to store?

●   What information do I want to get out of my database?

NB   You must also work out your answers to these two questions!!

Once you've decided what you are storing and what use you intend to make of the data, you are ready to start designing your database. Again, much of this can be done away from the computer.

What fields do you need?

You must break the data down into the smallest units you want to search or sort on. Each of these must be in a separate field.

If you were setting up **names**, you would probably break the name into three fields – *Title*, *Firstname* (or *Initials*) and *Surname*. This way you can sort the file into Surname order, or search for someone using the Firstname and Surname.

If you were storing **addresses**, you would probably want separate fields for Town/city, Region and/or Country. You can then sort your records into order on any of these fields, or locate records by specifying appropriate search criteria. For example, using Town/city and Country fields, you could search for addresses in Perth (Town/city), Australia (Country) rather than Perth (Town/city), Scotland (Country).

The number of lines in an address can vary considerably e.g. 12 High Street, Edinburgh, EH22 (with one address line before the

Tip

When planning your database, take a small sample of the data to be stored and examine it carefully. Break the detail on each item into small units for sorting and searching. You can then start to work out what fields will be needed to enable you to store all the necessary data for each item.

town) vs. The Old Schoolhouse, East Lane, Cranshaws, Nr Duns, Borders Region, TD10 (where you have 3 address lines before the town). When creating your tables set up enough fields to accommodate a full address (perhaps by using an Address 1, Address 2, and Address 3 field) before you get to the town, postcode etc. When entering data into address fields the Address 1 field should always be used, the Address 2 and Address 3 could be used if necessary. Make sure you always enter the town, postcode, county etc into the same field in each record.

How big are the fields?

You must also decide how much space is required for each field. The space you allocate must be long enough to accommodate the longest item that might go there. How long is the longest surname you want to store? If in doubt, take a sample of some typical names (McDonald, Peterson, MacKenzie, Harvey-Jones?) and add a few more characters to the longest one to be sure. An error in field size isn't as serious as an error in record structure as field sizes can be expanded without existing data being affected.

It is very important that you spend time organising and structuring your data before you start to computerise it – it'll save you a lot of time and frustration in the long run!

You can edit the structure of your table if necessary – but hunting through existing data to update records is time consuming, so it's best to get it right to start with!

Normalisation

When deciding on the tables required, you should consider how best to group the fields to minimise the duplication of data throughout the database – this is what is meant by the process of *normalisation*.

For example, you may be setting up a database to record details of items that you keep in stock and the suppliers that you use.

You could record all this information into one table, with fields for stock code, item description, cost, supplier name, supplier address, supplier telephone number, contact name, etc. However, using one table may result in a lot of data duplication – if you get 200 stock items from the same supplier, you would need to add the supplier details into the record for each stock item – that means that the suppler information would have to be entered 200 times!!

The solution to this kind of problem is to *normalise* the data. As a result of normalisation, you end up organising your data fields into a group of tables, that can be combined when and as required.

In the stock example, you could create two tables. One could hold details of the stock item, e.g. code, description, colour, supplier code, etc. The other could hold all the supplier information – supplier code, company name, contact name, address, telephone number, etc.

The information on each supplier would be entered once – into the supplier table. In the stock table, the supplier would be identified using the supplier code. The two tables could be linked through the supplier code, so that the data from both tables can be combined. So if you do have the same supplier for 200 stock items, you only need to enter the supplier details once!

There are several benefits to this approach:

● Each set of details (supplier) is stored (and therefore keyed in) only once.

● The stock table will be considerably smaller in size than it otherwise would have been.

● Should any of the supplier details change (phone number/address) you only have one record to update (in the Supplier table).

● If you wrongly identify a supplier in a record in the Stock table, you have only one field to correct in each record that contains the error, rather than several fields.

Take note

In page 25 we introduce a project (based around a company that sells holidays) that you can set up to help you learn how to use Access and practise the features that are introduced in this book. In the project the tables required and table structures have been worked out for you.

The project has been kept simple, as it would be impractical to discuss every table, form and report you might need in a book of this size. Although desirable in a real database, a booking system, a calendar to see what is booked when, a form of recording deposits and payments, etc. have not been included.

Getting into Access

It is assumed that Access is already installed on your computer. If it isn't, you must install it (or get someone else to install it for you) before going any further.

● If you are already working in another application, save any files that you want to keep, close the application(s) you are working in and return to the Desktop.

You're now ready to start using Access.

You can start Access through the Start Menu on the Taskbar or from the Microsoft Office Shortcut Bar (if you have it displayed).

❑ From the Taskbar

1 Click the Start button on the Taskbar.

2 Point to Programs.

3 Click on Microsoft Access.

4 Select Blank Database.

5 Click OK .

❑ From the Microsoft Office Shortcut Bar

6 Click the Microsoft Access tool 📖.

7 Complete steps 4 and 5 above.

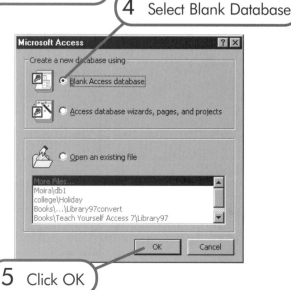

2 Point to Programs

3 Click on Access

4 Select Blank Database

1 Click Start

5 Click OK

The Access screen

Take note

Access, like other Office 2000 applications, personalise your menu and toolbars automatically. You can expand the menus to reveal all commands. After you select a command, or click a button on the toolbar, it appears on your personalised menu or toolbar. Toolbars can share space in a single row on the screen, so you have more room for your work.

Don't panic if your toolbars or menus are not exactly the same as those in the book!

Close the File New Database dialog box (click Cancel), so that you can view the Microsoft Access screen.

Looking at the Access screen, you can identify the standard elements of any Window: the Title bar, Menu bar and Toolbar; the Minimize, Maximize/Restore and Close buttons, and the Status bar.

I suggest you Maximize the Access application window. This way other windows that may be open on your desktop won't distract you.

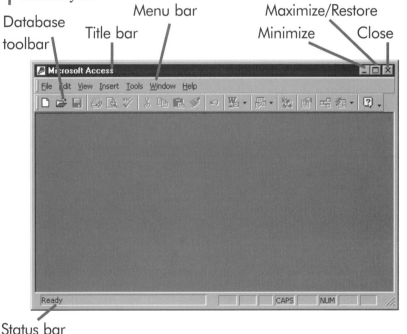

Status bar

Exiting Access

When you have completed your session in Access, you must exit the package and return to the Windows environment (*don't just switch off your computer!!*). To exit the package, click the Close button ⊠ on the Title Bar or open the **File** menu and choose **Exit**.

Summary

- ❏ A database is a collection of data.

- ❏ Access is a relational database.

- ❏ In a relational database, all related data is stored in one place.

- ❏ A relational database is organised into tables, records and fields.

- ❏ In Access, you will encounter various objects – tables, queries, forms, reports, pages, macros and modules.

- ❏ Preparation of your data is the first, very important step, in setting up your database.

- ❏ To get into Access, click Start, Programs, Microsoft Access.

- ❏ To get out of Access, click the Close button on the Application window, or choose Exit from the File menu.

2 Help

Office Assistant

When working in the Windows environment there is always plenty of help available. The trick is being able to find the help you need, when you need it. In this section, we look at the ways you can interrogate the on-line Help.

The default route into the on-line Help is through the Office Assistant. You may keep it open while you work – just drag it to a suitable area of the screen and leave it there.

To display its Help options (which vary depending on what you are doing), or to type in a question, simply give it a click!

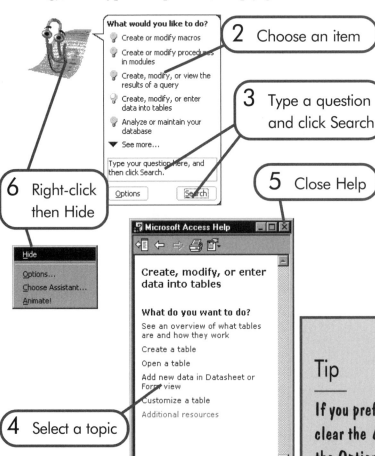

1 To display the Office Assistant press [F1].

or

Click the Office Assistant tool [?] .

2 Click an item in the list for Help on that topic.

or

3 Type in your question and click [Search]. A set of Help topics will appear on your screen.

4 Click on a topic to read it's Help page.

5 To close the Help, click ⊠ at the top right of the window.

❑ To hide the Assistant

6 Right-click on it and select Hide.

Tip

If you prefer to work without the Assistant, clear the *Use Office Assistant* checkbox on the Options tab. To restart it, choose *Show Office Assistant* from the Help menu.

14

Customising the Office Assistant

1 Click `Options` when the Office Assistant is displayed.

2 Select the Gallery tab.

3 Use `Next>` and `<Back` to see the personalities.

4 Click `OK` when you find the one that you want to use.

❑ Other options

5 Click `Options` as in step 1.

6 Select the Options tab.

7 Click the checkboxes to select or deselect the options as required.

8 Click `OK`.

You can customise the Office Assistant to take on a different 'personality' or to behave in the way you find most useful.

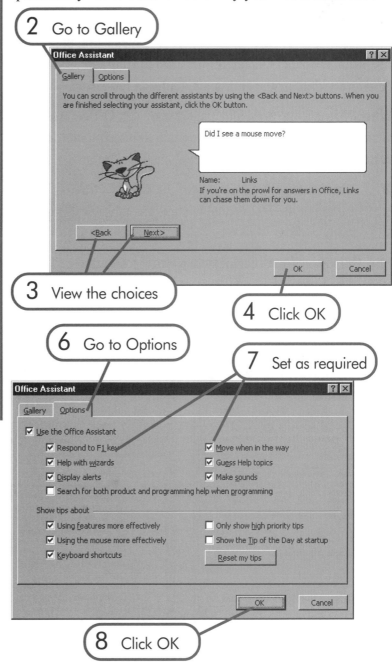

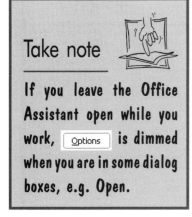

Take note

If you leave the Office Assistant open while you work, `Options` is dimmed when you are in some dialog boxes, e.g. Open.

15

On-line Help

Whether you opt to use Office Assistant or not, Help is presented through the on-line Help system.

The Help pages are displayed in a panel down the right side of your screen. When you access the Help pages using the Office Assistant, the panel displays either a list of Help topics you may be interested in, or the Help page that you requested.

When you access the Help pages with the Office Assistant switched off, the tabs that you can use to interrogate the Help system are also displayed.

Take note

Use the back ⇐ and Forward ⇒ tools to move through the pages you have viewed as necessary.

● You can toggle the display of the tabs by clicking ◄目 at the top of the Help panel to show the tabs, or 目► to hide them.

The Help pages can be located from the Contents, Answer Wizard or Index tabs.

Toggles display of tabs

Tabs from which you can interrogate the Help system

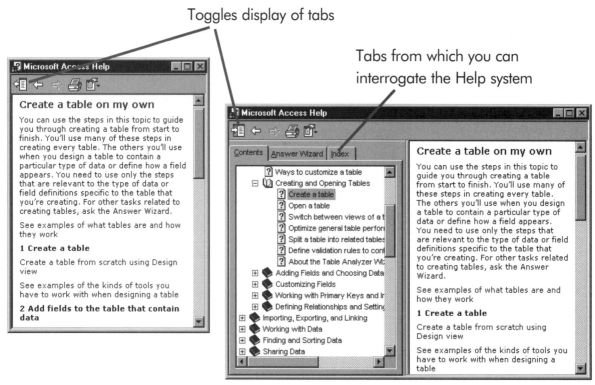

Basic steps

1 Click the + sign to the left of a folder that interests you.

2 Select a topic from the list displayed.

❑ The topic you select may contain links to other Help pages that could be useful

3 Work through the help system until you find the Help you need.

4 Close the Help system when you're finished.

Contents tab

The Contents tab displays a list of the Help folders available. You could browse through the folders to see what topics are included. You can easily explore any that appeal to you.

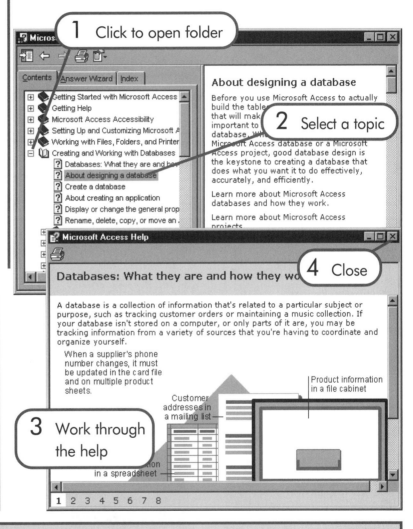

Take note

Click on a folder to display its contents; double-click to open or close it. Additional Help options are in the Options list.

Take note

If you've used the previous versions of Access, take a look in the Databases: General folder. You will find information on what's new in Access 2000.

Answer Wizard

The Answer Wizard offers an alternative route into the on-line Help pages.

The Help page you access may offer you links to other pages – explore any that are of interest.

Basic steps

1 Select the Answer Wizard tab.

2 Tell Access what you want to do.

3 Click Search.

4 Select a topic from the list presented.

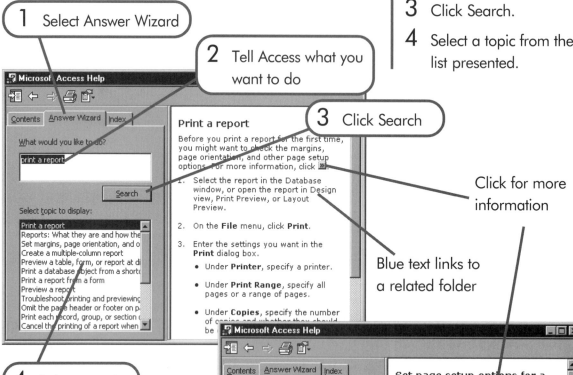

1 Select Answer Wizard

2 Tell Access what you want to do

3 Click Search

Click for more information

Blue text links to a related folder

4 Select a topic

Take note

If you find a Help page you wish to print, simply click 🖨 the print tool.

Basic steps

1 Select the Index tab.

2 Type the word(s) you're looking for or choose a keyword from the list.

3 Click Search.

4 Select a topic.

5 The Help page will be displayed.

The Index tab gives you quick access to ant topic and is particularly useful once you know what you are looking for!

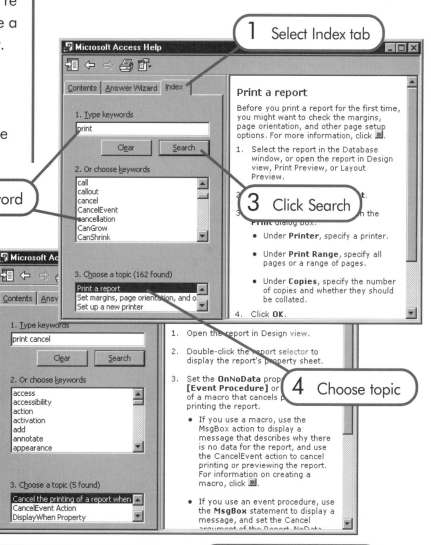

1 Select Index tab

2 Type or choose a word

3 Click Search

4 Choose topic

5 Help page displayed

Tip

Click Clear to delete the keywords if you want to do another search.

Take note

There more Help available on the Internet – select Office on the Web from the Help menu.

What's This?

If you are new to Microsoft Office applications or to the Windows interface, there will be many things on your screen that may puzzle you at first.

There may be strange looking tools on the toolbars; items listed in the menus may suggest things you've never heard of and other objects that appear and disappear as you work may add to your confusion!

Don't panic! If you don't know what it is – ask!

Basic steps

1 Hold down the [Shift] key and press [F1].

The mouse pointer looks like this.

❑ To find out what a particular tool does

2 Click the tool.

or

❑ To find out about an item in a menu list

3 Open the menu list by clicking on the menu name.

4 Click on the option required on the menu.

or

❑ To find out about anything else within the application window

5 Just click on it.

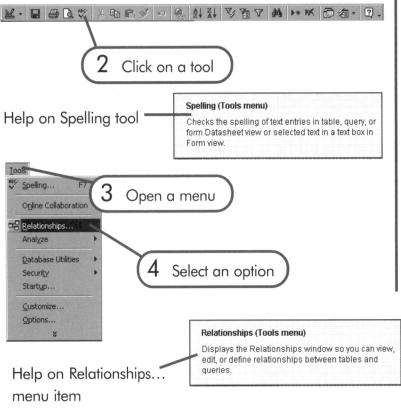

2 Click on a tool

Help on Spelling tool

Spelling (Tools menu)
Checks the spelling of text entries in table, query, or form Datasheet view or selected text in a text box in Form view.

3 Open a menu

4 Select an option

Relationships (Tools menu)
Displays the Relationships window so you can view, edit, or define relationships between tables and queries.

Help on Relationships... menu item

New
Creates a database object. Before clicking this button, in the Objects bar click the type of database object you want to create.

Help on the New button on the Database window toolbar

Basic steps

1 Open the Tools menu.
2 Choose Customize...
3 Select the Options tab in the Customize dialog box.
4 Select the Show shortcut keys in ScreenTips option.
5 Click Close.
6 Point to a tool on the toolbar – if it has a shortcut key it will be displayed with the ScreenTip.

ScreenTips

If you point to any tool on a displayed toolbar, a ScreenTip appears to describe the function of the tool.

If you like using keyboard shortcuts, you can customise the ScreenTips to display the shortcut as well. This will help you learn the shortcuts quickly.

Here's how to toggle the keyboard shortcut display on the ScreenTips.

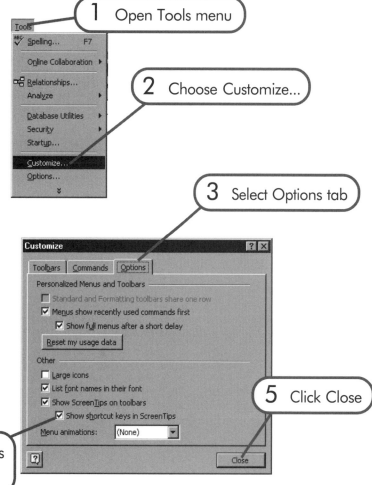

1 Open Tools menu

2 Choose Customize...

3 Select Options tab

5 Click Close

4 Select/deselect as required

Take note

Right-click on any toolbar and choose Customize... from the shortcut menu to display the Customize dialog box.

Summary

- ❑ Press [F1] or click the Office Assistant tool to get Help with your tasks.

- ❑ The appearance and behaviour of the Office Assistant can be modified.

- ❑ The Office Assistant can be switched off if you prefer.

- ❑ The on-line Help can be interrogated from the Contents, Answer Wizard or Index tabs in the Help system.

- ❑ If you have Internet access you can visit Office on the Web – a useful, regularly updated site.

- ❑ What's This? is activated by [Shift]-[F1]. Just click on a tool or menu item to find out more about it.

- ❑ ScreenTips are useful learning aids when you start out using Access.

3 Building a database

Creating a new database

The first thing we have to do is create a database for our data, and give it a suitable name.

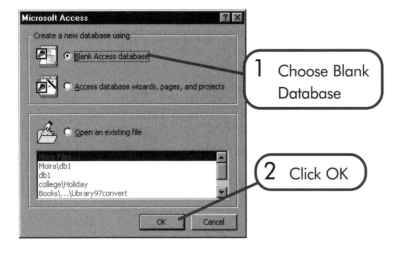

1 Choose Blank Database

2 Click OK

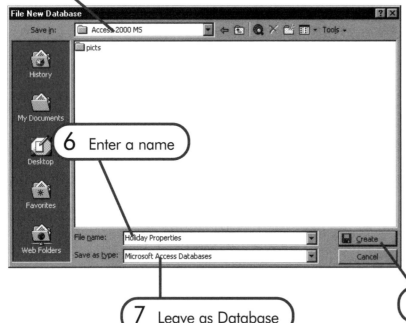

5 Select the folder

6 Enter a name

7 Leave as Database

8 Click Create

❑ On starting Access

1 Choose Blank Data-base at the Microsoft Access dialog box.

2 Click OK .

❑ From within Access

3 Open the File menu and choose New or click 🗋.

4 Choose Database from the General Tab and click OK .

5 At the File New Data-base dialog box, select the folder you wish to store the database in.

6 Enter a File name. Here it is called *Holiday Properties*.

7 Leave the Save as type: field at Microsoft Access Databases.

8 Click 🖫 Create .

The project

The next sections describe a project that you may like to work through. It is deliberately simple, but demonstrates many of the Access features you need to get to grips with. You have set up a travel service that has an extensive database of quality accommodation.

Your clients will contact you with details of:
- where they want to go;
- when they want to go;
- how many people need to be accommodated;
- what kind of board (e.g. self-catering) is required.

You can interrogate your database to get a list of properties that match their requirements and check prices. If a client wants to make a booking, you can get owner's name, address and telephone number, and contact them to arrange the let.

Your Holiday Database will consist of four tables:
- **Type of Accommodation** e.g. cottage, flat or room;
- **Accommodation details,** e.g. location, number of beds, whether it has a garden/pool/maid service;
- one with **Price** details;
- one with details of the property owner or **Contact.**

We'll set up a **Type of Accommodation** and a **Contacts** table in this chapter.

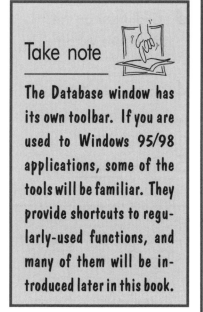

Take note

The Database window has its own toolbar. If you are used to Windows 95/98 applications, some of the tools will be familiar. They provide shortcuts to regularly-used functions, and many of them will be introduced later in this book.

Database toolbar

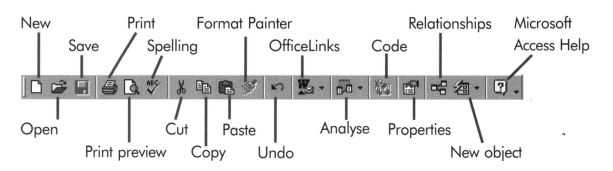

New
Save
Print
Spelling
Format Painter
OfficeLinks
Code
Relationships
Microsoft Access Help
Open
Print preview
Cut
Copy
Paste
Undo
Analyse
Properties
New object

Creating a new table

The data you store will be held in a table (or tables). A table consists of:

● the record **structure**, that is, the field names, data types, descriptions and field properties;

and

● the record **data**, for example, accommodation details, price details, contact details.

Give careful consideration to your table structure. It can be edited (you can add fields, delete fields and change the field properties) at a later stage, but things are a lot easier if you get it right to begin with.

You must decide:

● what **fields** you require in your table;

● what kind of data will go in each field, i.e. text, date, number, etc.;

● which field will be your **primary key** field – one that uniquely identifies the record, e.g. property code, product code, employee reference number.

Once you've worked out the structure, you can then create your table.

Basic steps

1 Ensure that Tables is selected in the Objects bar in the database window.

2 Double-click Create table in Design View.

or

3 Click New on the Database window toolbar.

4 At the New Table dialog box, choose Design View.

5 Click  OK .

Tip

Good planning at the start is the secret of good databases. Be clear about what you want to store and what you intend to do with the data once it's stored.

Take note

You can also create a new table if you click the drop-down arrow beside **the New Object** tool on the Database window Toolbar and choose **Table**.

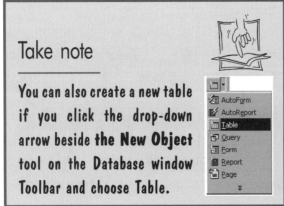

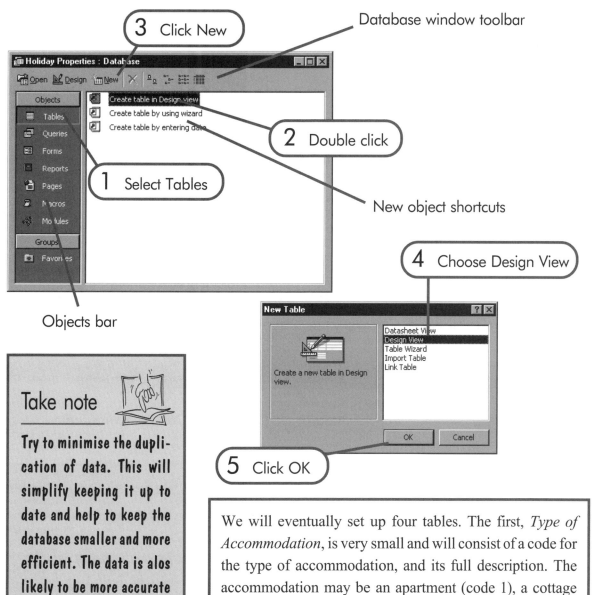

3 Click New

Database window toolbar

2 Double click

1 Select Tables

New object shortcuts

Objects bar

4 Choose Design View

5 Click OK

Take note

Try to minimise the duplication of data. This will simplify keeping it up to date and help to keep the database smaller and more efficient. The data is alos likely to be more accurate if you don't have to enter the same thing several times.

We will eventually set up four tables. The first, *Type of Accommodation*, is very small and will consist of a code for the type of accommodation, and its full description. The accommodation may be an apartment (code 1), a cottage (code 2), a flat (code 3) or a room (code 4). This must be set up before the *Accommodation* table. The *Accommodation* table will eventually hold the type of accommodation code, which will be used to look up the full description in the *Type of Accommodation* table.

Table Design window

The Table Design window has two panes – one that lets you specify the field name, data type and description, and the other where you can specify the field properties.

You can use the **Field Properties** pane to customise the format of the field you are defining. The amount of customisation permitted depends on the data type selected for the field, for example:

- the number of characters in a Text field;
- the format of the date in a Date/Time field;
- the decimal accuracy of a Number field;
- whether Duplicate entries are permitted in a field.

We'll consider some of the properties in the next pages.

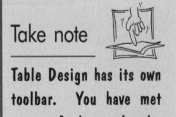

Take note

Table Design has its own toolbar. You have met some of these already; others will be introduced in the next few sections.

Table Design toolbar

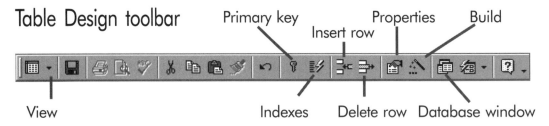

Primary key   Properties   Build

Insert row

View   Indexes   Delete row   Database window

Type of Accommodation table

The first table we will create will hold details of the accommodation type – its code and description. This detail will be looked up from the *Accommodation* table.

Detail on the structure of the table is given below:

Take note

Any table storing data that will be looked up by another table must be set up *before* the one that will do the looking up.

Field Name	Data Type	Format /Field size	Other field properties/Notes
AccCode	Number	Long Integer	Primary key
Description	Text	20	

Number data type

Basic steps

1 Type in the first Field Name in your table – *AccCode*.

2 Press [Tab], or point and click, to move to the Data Type.

3 Click the down arrow to display the list of data types.

4 Choose the type – Number in this case.

5 Press [Tab] and in the Description column, type the message to be shown in the Status bar when data is entered in this field. If you don't want a message, leave it blank.

6 Press [Tab] to move to the Field Name column for your next field.

In a field with a **Number** data type, you can specify the accuracy of the number that can be entered by setting the **Field Size** property. For the *AccCode* field leave the Field Size at the default – Long Integer. This table will eventually be related to the *Accommodation* table through this field.

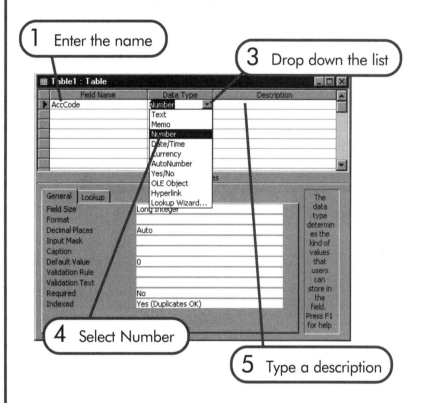

Take note

Each field must have a field name and data type.

Take note

Field names can be up to 64 characters in length and can include any combination of text, numbers, spaces and special characters, except for the full stop (.), exclamation mark (!), accent grave (`) and square brackets ([ ]).

Text data type

The next field is the accommodation description field. This field is a text field that will hold the accommodation description – apartment, cottage, flat or room. 20 characters will be more than long enough for this field.

The Field Size is set in the **Field Properties** pane. Pressing [F6] switches between the upper and lower panes.

1 Type in the Field Name – *Description*.

2 Set the Data Type to Text.

3 Enter a Description if you wish.

4 Press [F6] to move to the lower pane.

5 Change the Field Size property to 20.

6 Press [F6] to return to the upper pane.

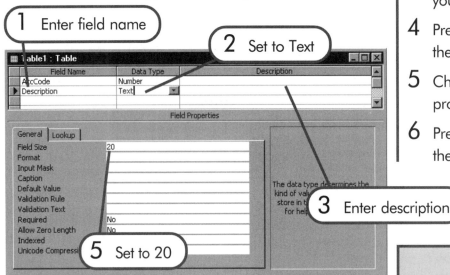

1 Enter field name

2 Set to Text

3 Enter description

5 Set to 20

6 Press [F6]

Tip

Keep field names short and easy to remember!

Take note

In text fields the default size is 50 characters. If a field size proves too small, it can be extended later up to a maximum of 255.

Take note

The Unicode Compression property is present in Text, Memo and Hyperlink fields. To minimise the storage space taken up by your database, leave this option at Yes (the default). See Tables: Field Properties in the on-line Help for more information.

Basic steps

1 To select a single field to become your primary key, click anywhere inside the field row in the upper pane.

2 Click the primary key tool 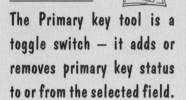 on the toolbar.

❑ Note the key icon that appears to the left of the key field(s).

Primary key

Once you have completed specifying your table structure, and edited any fields you want to change, you should indicate which field is to be your primary key. The primary key is a field (or combination of fields) that uniquely identifies each record in your table.

If you don't specify the primary key, Access can set one up when you first save your design. It will set up a field called *ID* with an AutoNumber data type if you do this.

We will specify the *AccCode* field as our Primary key.

Take note

The Primary key tool is a toggle switch — it adds or removes primary key status to or from the selected field.

Key icon   1 Select the field

Table1 : Table

Field Name	Data Type	Description
AccCode	Number	
Description	Text	

Field Properties

General | Lookup

Field Size	Long Integer
Format	
Decimal Places	Auto
Input Mask	
Caption	
Default Value	0
Validation Rule	
Validation Text	
Required	No
Indexed	Yes (No Duplicates)

A field name can be up to 64 characters long, including spaces. Press F1 for help on field names.

Take note

To select several fields to become your primary key, hold the [Ctrl] key down as you click the row selector bar — the grey bar down the left-hand side of the field names for each field.

If you choose the wrong field (or fields) to be your primary key, simply select the correct one (or ones) and click the primary key tool.

Saving the design

When you have the table design specified, you must **save** it. Once the design has been saved, you can:

● close the table (and the database) and leave data entry till later; or

● move into the Datasheet View, so you can enter data straight away (see Chapter 6).

At this stage, I suggest you close the table and leave data entry for Chapter 6.

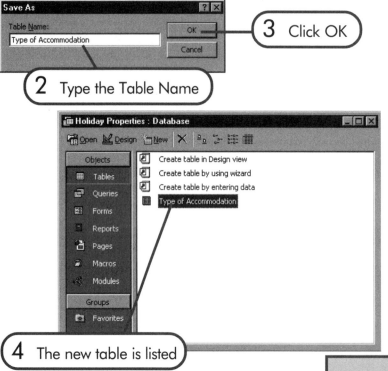

2 Type the Table Name

3 Click OK

4 The new table is listed

5 Click View tool

6 Choose Datatsheet View

Basic steps

1 Click the Save tool 🔲.

2 At the Save As dialog box, enter *Type of Accommodation* as the Table Name.

3 Click [OK].

❑ Enter data later

4 Click 🗵 to close the Design window. At the Database window, the new table is listed on the Tables tab.

❑ Go to Datasheet View

5 Click the View tool 🎬 on the Table Design tolbar.

Or

6 Click View tool's arrow and choose Datasheet View. You arrive in Datasheet View ready for data entry.

Take note

Once your table design has been saved, clicking the Save tool 🔲 will record to disk any changes you make.

Basic steps

1 Select Tables in the Objects Bar on the left of the database window.

2 Double -click Create table by using wizard.

3 At the Table Wizard dialog box, select the category of Table – in our case Business.

4 Choose *Contacts* from the Sample Tables list.

Table Wizard

Instead of specifying your table design from scratch, you might find Table Wizard useful for some tables. We'll use it to set up our *Contacts* table for the Holiday Properties database.

Contacts table

This table will contain the names and addresses of the people who either own or manage the properties on our lists.

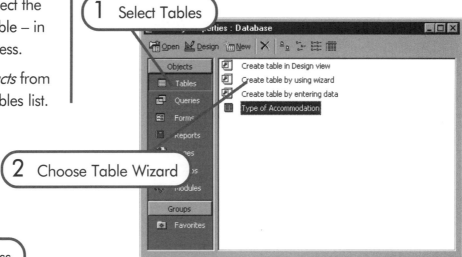

1 Select Tables

2 Choose Table Wizard

3 Select Business

4 Choose Contacts

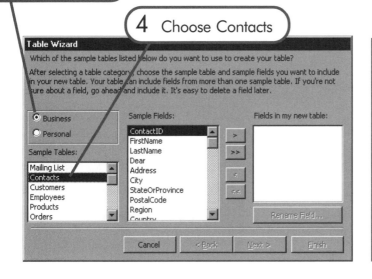

Take note

You could create a new table using a wizard by clicking New at the top of the Database window, then double clicking Table Wizard in the dialog box.

Specifying the fields

Using the table on page 35 as a guide, select the fields you want to use in your *Contacts* table. It is essentially a name and address table for our property owners/contacts.

When adding fields to the **Fields in my new table** list, the field name can be changed (e.g. *State* to *County*).

1 Select the field from the Sample Fields list.

2 Click the Add field button [>] to add the field to the Fields in my new table list.

3 If you add a field by mistake, select it and click [<].

❑ Renaming a field

4 Select it in the Fields in my new table list.

5 Click [Rename Field...].

6 Key in the new name.

7 Click [OK].

8 Continue until you've added all the fields then click [Next>].

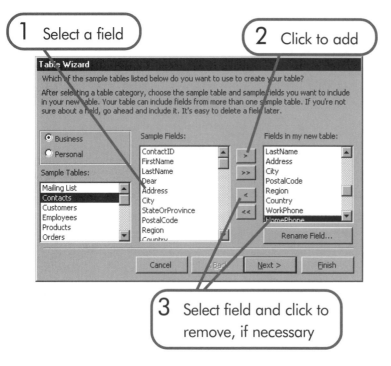

1 Select a field

2 Click to add

3 Select field and click to remove, if necessary

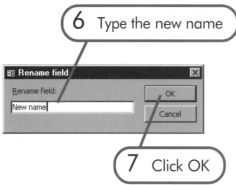

6 Type the new name

7 Click OK

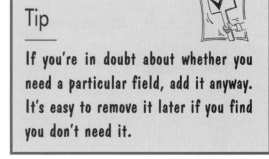

Tip

If you're in doubt about whether you need a particular field, add it anyway. It's easy to remove it later if you find you don't need it.

Contacts table

Field Name	Notes
ContactID	Primary Key – specifying this comes AFTER the fields are set up
FirstName	Set up using a Table Wizard therefore field properties picked up from Wizard
LastName	Set up using a Table Wizard therefore field properties picked up from Wizard
Address	Set up using a Table Wizard therefore field properties picked up from Wizard
City	Set up using a Table Wizard therefore field properties picked up from Wizard
State	This field name is changed to County during set up process
PostalCode	Check the field properties once the design is complete. ✳
Country	Set up using a Table Wizard therefore field properties picked up from Wizard
WorkPhone	Check the field properties once the design is complete. ✳
HomePhone	Check the field properties once the design is complete.✳

✳ *Things like Input Masks will need to be edited or deleted as they follow the American conventions. Input masks are patterns which limit the range of characters that can be entered into a field (see pages 46–47 for more).*

Take note

If you add a field by mistake, select it in the **Fields in my new table** list and click the [<] button.

The [>>] button adds all the sample fields to the **Fields in my new table** list.

The [<<] button removes all the fields from this list.

Finishing off

Once you have specified the field names for your table, the next step is to name the table and set the Primary Key.

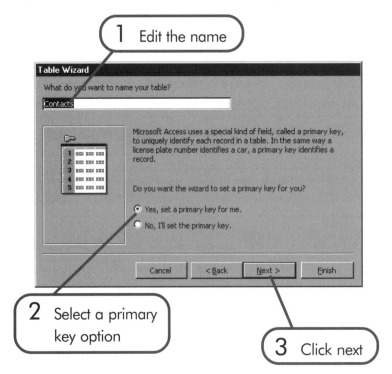

1 Edit the name

Table Wizard

What do you want to name your table?

Contacts

Microsoft Access uses a special kind of field, called a primary key, to uniquely identify each record in a table. In the same way a license plate number identifies a car, a primary key identifies a record.

Do you want the wizard to set a primary key for you?

○ Yes, set a primary key for me.

○ No, I'll set the primary key.

| Cancel | < Back | Next > | Finish |

2 Select a primary key option

3 Click next

1 Edit the table name if necessary.

2 Specify whether Access or you will set the primary key. Leave it to Access – it sets the *ContactID* field as the primary key, with an AutoNumber data type.

If you choose No I'll set the primary key, then click Next, Access requests additional information about the type of data the primary key will hold.

3 Click .

Take note

ContactID in the *Contacts* and the *Accommodation* tables will be the fields through which the tables are related. You can make this relationship at the end.

Take note

If you click the Finish button once you have added all the fields to your database, the wizard will give the table the default table name and set the ContactID field as the primary key (with an AutoNumber data type). It will also take you straight into Datasheet View.

Checking relationships

1 Select the table with the relationship you want to check or change.

2 Click ⟦ Relationships... ⟧.

3 The current type of relationship is shown in the Relationships dialog box. Select the first option listed for this relation.

4 Click ⟦ OK ⟧.

5 Once you are satisfied that the relationships are OK, click ⟦ Next> ⟧.

Normally, if a database contains more than one table, each table is related to at least one other. However, the *Contacts* table is not related to the *Type of Accommodation* table that we have already set up.

Table Wizard displays a list of the tables in your database, and indicates whether or not they are related. (In some cases the Wizard makes the relationship between tables automatically.)

The dialog box should state that the *Contacts* table is not related to the *Type of Accommodation* table.

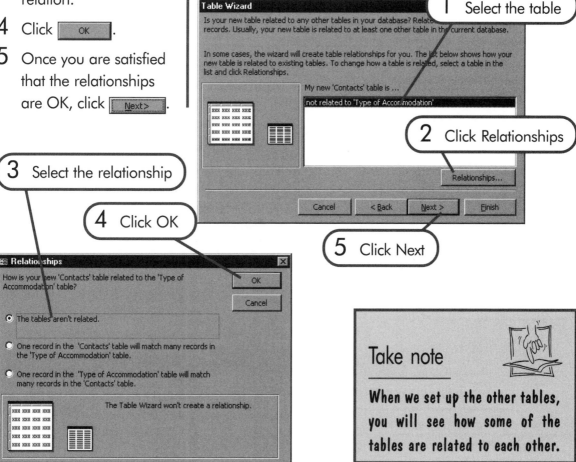

Take note

When we set up the other tables, you will see how some of the tables are related to each other.

Leaving Table Wizard

The last step is to choose where to go next.

- **Modify the table design** takes you to the Design window to modify the structure. We need to do this. *Postal Code*, *WorkPhone* and *HomePhone* fields all have Input Masks in American formats. These should be deleted, so we can input data in our format.

- **Enter data directly into the table** takes you to the Datasheet View. This is the default option.

- **Enter data into the table using a form the wizard creates for me** – the Wizard will design a simple form that shows one record at a time. You can use the form or datasheet to input, edit and view records.

Basic steps

1 Select Modify the table design.

2 Click **Finish**.

3 At the Table Design window select a field to be modified.

4 Press [F6].

5 Delete the entry in the Input Mask row.

6 Press [F6].

❑ Repeat for all fields as needed, then save the edited design and close the Table Design window.

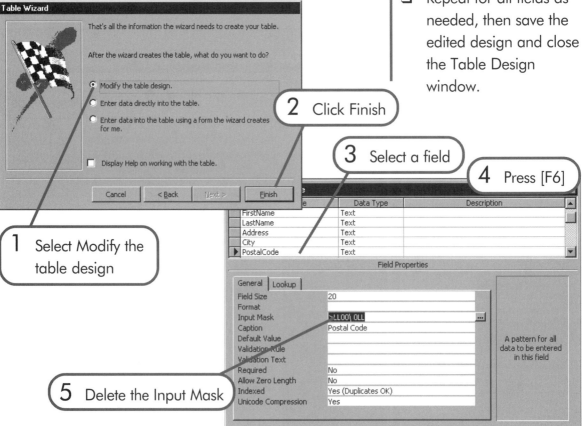

1 Select Modify the table design

2 Click Finish

3 Select a field

4 Press [F6]

5 Delete the Input Mask

38

Basic steps

1 Click the Close button
   ⊠ on the Database
   window.

❑ Your database is
   closed, but you are still
   in Access.

Closing a database

If you've finished working on your database, you might want to close it. You can close a database without leaving Access. If you exit Access, any open databases are closed as part of the exit routine.

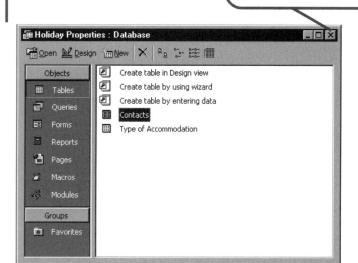

1 Close the database

Take note

You can't exit from the Design View without being reminded to save your design if you haven't done so already.

If you don't want to save, choose NO at the prompt that appears.

Tip

Save your table design regularly as you work (this is particularly important with larger tables) — don't leave it till the end.

If there's a power failure, or your computer crashes and the design hasn't been saved, it will be lost and you'll have to start all over again.

If you save regularly and such a disaster befalls you, at least you'll have the design as it was at the last save.

Summary

- [ ] To create a new database, click the New Database tool ☐ on the Database toolbar.

- [ ] To create a new table, select Tables in the Objects bar in the Database window and click New.

- [ ] Each field *must* have a Field Name and a Data Type.

- [ ] Number and Text data types are introduced in this section.

- [ ] Each table should have a unique field (or fields) set as the primary key.

- [ ] You should save your table design regularly as you build it up (click the Save tool 🖫 on the Design toolbar).

- [ ] To close your table design and return to the Database window, click the Close button ☒.

- [ ] To change from Design View to Datasheet View in your Table, click the View tool ▦.

- [ ] You can quickly set up the structure of some tables using a Table Wizard.

- [ ] To close a database, but remain in Access, click the close button on the Database window.

4 Data types

Opening a database

A database must be open before you can do any work on it. If you closed your database at the end of the last chapter, open it again so that you can set up the next table.

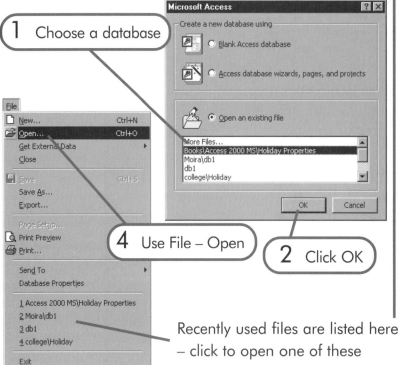

1 Choose a database

4 Use File – Open

2 Click OK

Recently used files are listed here – click to open one of these

❑ As you go into Access

1 Select the database from the dialog box.

2 Click OK.

❑ From within Access

3 Click 🖙 on the Database toolbar.

Or

4 Choose Open from the File menu.

5 At the Open dialog box, choose the database.

6 Double-click on the file or click 🖙 Open ▾.

In a multiuser environment, use the Open options to limit access to the database.

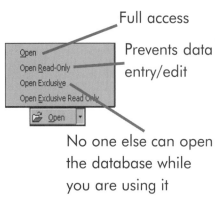

Full access

Prevents data entry/edit

No one else can open the database while you are using it

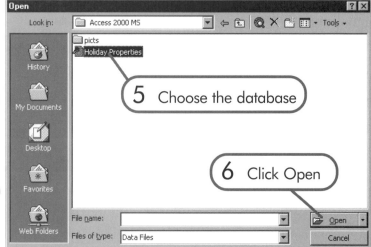

5 Choose the database

6 Click Open

Adding a new table

Create a new table as shown on page 26, then move to the Table Design window to define the first field.

This next table is much larger than the previous one, and needs to use many different data types in its structure. A summary of the fields and their properties is shown on page 44. Full instructions will be given to help you set up each new data type. Check the data types and properties of the fields overleaf to help you complete the table accurately.

Accommodation table

The *Accommodation* table will hold details of the holiday accommodation we have on offer.

● Board is self-catering (SC), bed and breakfast (BB) or half board (HB).

● Properties may have a swimming pool, maid service or garden.

● Prices depend on the time of year.

● The type of accommodation – apartment (1), cottage (2), flat (3) or room (4) will be 'looked up' in the *Type of Accommodation* table.

● A photograph of the accommodation will be included in this table.

● Information on the area surrounding our properties, e.g. places to visit, good eating and drinking houses. This is available as Word document files. We will set up a 'hyperlink' field in this table to link to these files as appropriate.

Accommodation table

Field Name	Data Type	Format/ Field size	Other field properties/ Notes
Reference	AutoNumber[1]		Primary Key. Indexed (No Duplicates)
Season Start	Date/Time[2]	Short date	Input Mask 99/99/00
Season End	Date/Time[2]	Short date	Input Mask 99/99/00
Country	Text	20	Indexed
Board	Text	2	Validation rule ="SC" or ="BB" or ="HB"
AccCode	Lookup[3]		
Swimming Pool	Yes/No[4]	Yes/No	
Maid Service	Yes/No[4]	Yes/No	Default Value = Yes
Garden	Yes/No[4]	Yes/No	
Price Range	Text	1	Description: Enter Code A-E Validation rule ="A" or ="B" or ="C" or ="D" or ="E"
Sleeps	Number	Long Integer	Default Value = 4
ContactID	Number	Long integer	Required = YES
Notes	Memo[5]		For information specific to the property, not covered by the other fields
Picture	OLE Object[6]		For a photograph of the property
General	Hyperlink[7]		To link to Word documents

Data Types

[1] AutoNumber page 45
[2] Date/Time page 47
[3] Lookup page 51
[4] Yes/No page 53
[5] Memo page 55
[6] OLE Object page 55
[7] Hyperlink page 56

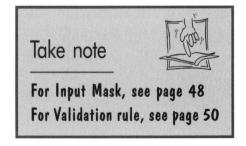

Take note

For Input Mask, see page 48
For Validation rule, see page 50

44

AutoNumber

1 Type in the first Field Name.

2 Choose AutoNumber in the Data Type column.

3 Enter a Description if you wish.

4 Make this field your primary key – click .

5 Press [Tab] to move to the Field Name column for your next field.

Take note

When specifying a field's properties, ensure that your insertion point is inside the correct Field in the upper pane, before you press [F6] to move to the lower pane. The current field is clearly indicated by the black triangle in the selector column, to the left of the field name.

Our first field will contain the accommodation reference. This will be the unique identifier for each property – no two will have the same reference. The field could be called something like *Reference* or *Accommodation Code*.

Fields that are used as identification fields in this way can be completed automatically by Access if the reference field is given an **AutoNumber** data type. When you enter data into the finished table, Access puts 1 in the *Reference* field in the first record, 2 in the second, 3 in the third and so on. You *cannot* enter data into the field, and Access never uses the same number twice (even if records are added and deleted later), so the field is always unique.

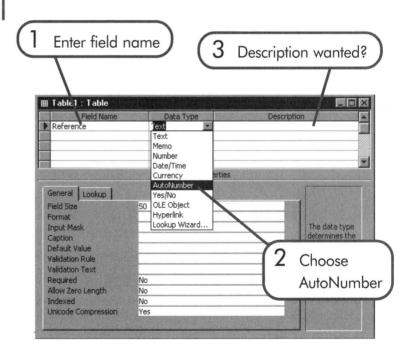

With an AutoNumber data type, you can specify up to five field properties (see next page).

Field size

Use the smallest practical field size. Smaller sizes can be processed faster and require less memory. Long Integer is the default option for AutoNumber and Number fields.

New values

Leave this set at *Increment* to have the reference automatically incremented by 1 at each new record.

Format

You can specify the number format for the AutoNumber field. You can select from the drop-down list of pre-set formats, or specify your own format.

To define a format, key the number pattern into the Format field. Characters that can be used include:

0   a digit or 0   .   the decimal separator

a digit or nothing   "”"   a literal (something that actually appears in the field)

Other permitted user characters are listed in the on-line Help under **Format Property**.

Caption

In the Caption field, you can type the label to appear beside the field when it is inserted into a **form**. (We will deal with forms in Chapter 10.) A caption can be more user-friendly than a field name. If we use a field name like *Ref*, a suitable Caption might be 'Accommodation Code'.

Indexed

Indexing fields can speed up searches (although updates are slower). If a field is designated the **Primary Key** this property is automatically set to *Yes, (No Duplicates)*. Index fields that you want to sort or search on, as it speeds up the operations.

Take note

The Format property option also appears in fields that have a Text data type.

The Caption property option is present for all data types.

The Indexed property option is present for all data types except Memo, OLE and Hyperlink.

Indexed fields have either 'No Duplicates' or 'Duplicates OK' status. 'No Duplicates' ensures that the value in the field is unique. 'Duplicates OK' allows non-unique values to be entered.

Date/Time

1 Type *Season Start* as the Field Name.

2 For the Data Type select Date/Time.

3 Press [F6] to switch to the Field Properties pane.

4 Click the drop-down arrow to display the list of Format options.

5 Choose Short Date.

6 Press [F6] to return to the upper pane.

7 Key in a Description if required (e.g. *Only needed if not open all year*).

❑ Set up the *Season End* field in the same way.

At our *Season Start* and *Season End* fields we are going to specify a Date/Time data type.

We will specify the format the date will take as DD/MM/YY (e.g. 01/06/97) – what Access calls a Short Date format. This is specified in the Field Properties pane.

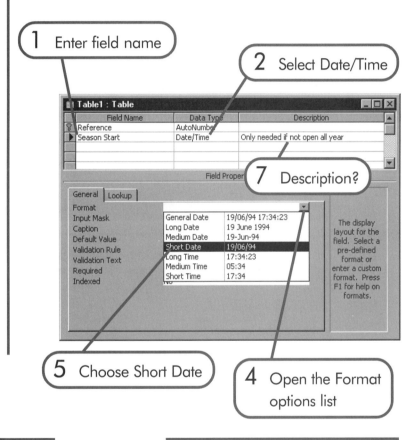

1 Enter field name

2 Select Date/Time

7 Description?

5 Choose Short Date

4 Open the Format options list

Sample date formats:

Short - 12/10/99

Medium - 12-Oct-99

Long - 12-October-1999

Take note

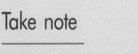

Date formats follow the Regional Setting Properties specified in the Control Panel in Windows 95/98.

Input Mask

Regardless of how you choose to display your date, you will want to make sure that the date is keyed in accurately.

Different people might key in the same date with different separators between the day, month and year. 12/06/99, 12:06:99, 12-06-99 or 12.06.99 may all mean the 12th of June 1999 to us, but Access might not be so sure! To help ensure that data entry is completed correctly, you can specify an Input Mask, or pattern, the data should take.

● The Input Mask does not affect the display Format.

Go back to the *Season Start* field to set up an Input Mask.

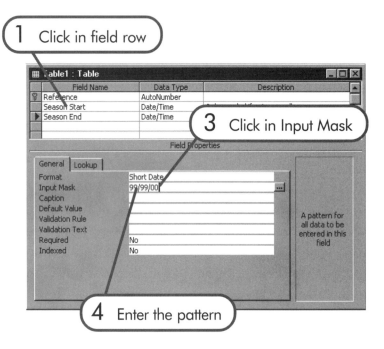

● When you enter data into these fields, an underscore will appear to indicate the position for each digit, and the slash character will be in place between the day, month and year sections (__/__/__) – it will not be necessary to key in the slash at data entry.

1 Put the insertion point in the *Season Start* field in the upper pane.

2 Press [F6] to move to the lower pane.

3 Move to the Input Mask field.

4 Key in the pattern 99/99/00 (see table opposite).

5 Press [F6] to return to the upper pane.

❑ Do the same for the *Season End* field.

Tip

You can use a Wizard to help you build your Input Mask. To try it, click the Build button 📖 to the right of the Input Mask property field. If you use the Wizard, all three parts of the Input Mask are specified.

Input Mask patterns

When setting up your pattern, you use special characters to show the type of input allowed, and whether or not input is required. These are listed here.

0	Digit (0-9). Entry required. Plus (+) and Minus (-) signs not allowed.
9	Digit or space. Entry not required. Plus and Minus signs not allowed.
#	Digit or space. Entry not required. Plus and Minus signs allowed.
L	Letter (A-Z). Entry required.
?	Letter (A-Z). Entry not required.
A	Letter or digit. Entry required.
a	Letter or digit. Entry not required.
&	Any character or a space. Entry required.
C	Any character or a space. Entry not required.
<	Causes all characters that follow to be converted to lower case.
>	Causes all characters that follow to be converted to upper case.
!	Causes Input Mask to fill from right to left when characters on the left side are optional.
\	Causes the following character to be displayed as the literal character, not interpreted as a mask code character, i.e. \L is displayed as L, and doesn't mean Letter (A-Z).

An Input Mask can contain up to three parts, each part being separated from the others using a semi-colon i.e. 99/99/00;0;_

- The first part, 99/99/00, specifies the Input Mask itself.

- The second part specifies whether any literal display characters are stored with the data. 0 means that they are; 1 means that only data is stored. The default is 0.

- The third part specifies the character used to display spaces in the Input Mask. The default character is the underline. If you want to use a space, enclose it in quotes i.e. 99/99/00;0; " "

Indexed property

As the *Country*, *Board*, *Price Range* and *Type of Accommodation* fields may be used in sorts and queries, they should be indexed with duplicates allowed.

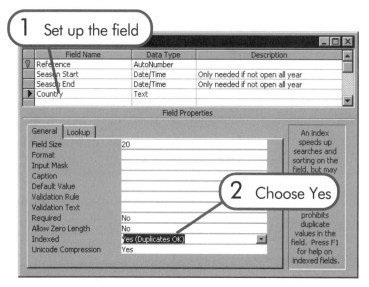

Validation Rule property

Validation rules ensure that only the valid data is entered. The *Board* field should only accept one of these codes – SC (self-catering), BB (bed & breakfast) or HB (half board).

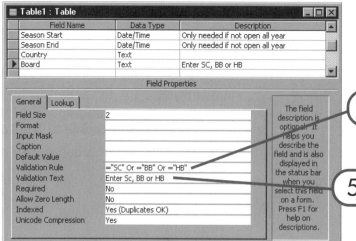

❏ Indexed property

1 Set up the *Country* field as a Text field, setting the size to 20.

2 Set Indexed to Yes (Duplicates OK).

❏ Validation Rule

3 Set up the *Board* field as a text field, Size 2.

4 In the Validation Rule field enter =*"SC"* or =*"BB"* or =*"HB"*.

5 Type the Validation Text to appear if the rule is not met.

❏ Set up the *Price Range* field, Size 1, with a Validation Rule of =*"A"* or =*"B"* or =*"C"* or =*"D"* or =*"E"*.

Basic steps

1 Enter the Field Name –
  AccCode.

2 In the Data Type field,
  choose Lookup
  Wizard... Work
  through it, clicking
  [Next>] after each
  step and [Finish] at
  the end.

3 At the first step, choose
  *I want the lookup
  column to look up the
  values...*

4 Select the table or
  query that contains the
  data (if you're working
  through this project you
  want *Type of Accom-
  modation*).

                                cont...

We will set up the *AccCode* as a Lookup field. The data for a
Lookup field is stored in another table, and looked up as
necessary. The advantages of using a Lookup field are:

●   The actual data needs to be keyed in only once;

●   The table receiving the data is easier to read as it contains
    fewer visible codes.

This field will look up the *Type of Accommodation* table for
its data.

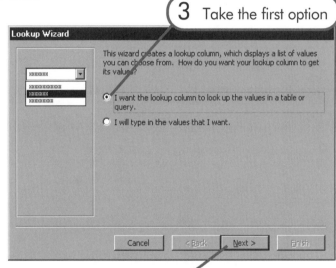

3 Take the first option

Click Next after each step

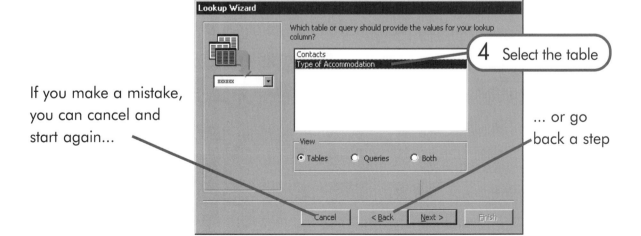

4 Select the table

If you make a mistake,
you can cancel and
start again...

... or go
back a step

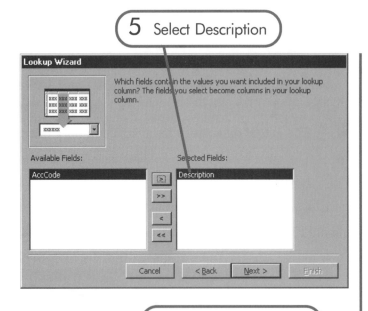

5 Select Description

cont...

5 Select the field containing the values to be looked up – *Description* in our case.

6 Leave the Hide key column ticked.

7 The chequered flag marks the end! Edit the column label if you want something other than that suggested, e.g. *Type of Accommodation.*

8 Click Finish.

❑ When prompted to save your table, choose Yes. At the Save As dialog box, name it *Accommodation*, and click   OK .

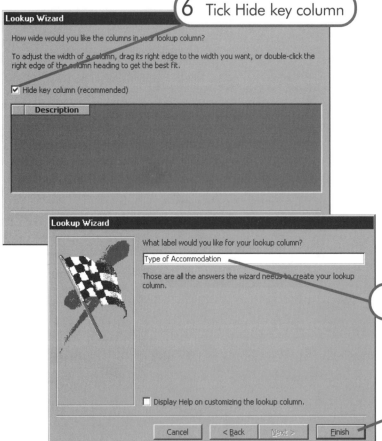

6 Tick Hide key column

7 Edit the label

8 Click Finish to end

Basic steps

1 Type in the Field Name – *Swimming Pool.*

2 Set the Data Type to Yes/No.

❏ Set up the *Maid Service* and *Garden* fields in the same way.

❏ Default value

3 Place the insertion point in the *Maid Service* field.

4 Press [F6] and in the Default Value field, type *Yes.*

❏ Set up the *Sleeps* field with a Number data type and a Default Value of 4.

❏ Required (see page 54)

5 Set up the *ContactID* field with a Number data type.

6 Press [F6] and set the Field Size to Long Integer.

7 Set the Required property option to Yes.

If a field can have one of two values in it, e.g. *Yes* or *No*, *True* or *False*, *On* or *Off*, choose the **Yes/No** data type. The next three fields – Swimming Pool, Maid Service and Garden – are all Yes/No fields.

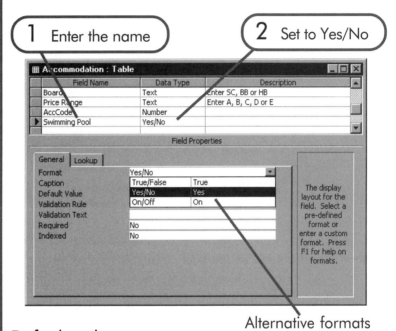

1 Enter the name

2 Set to Yes/No

Alternative formats

Default value

The default value in a Yes/No field is *No*. As we know that most of our holiday accommodation has Maid Service, we can change the default value to *Yes* by typing *Yes* in the Default Value field of the lower pane for that field.

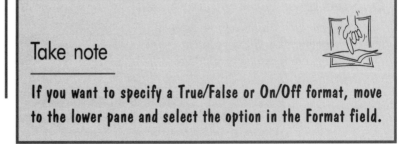

Take note

If you want to specify a True/False or On/Off format, move to the lower pane and select the option in the Format field.

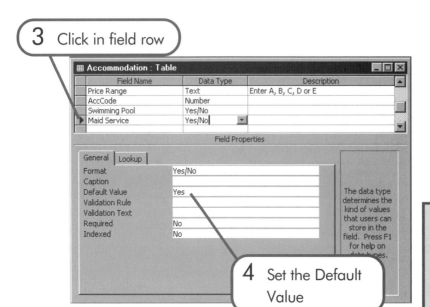

3 Click in field row

4 Set the Default Value

Required property

As the *ContactID* field will be used to link the *Accommodation* table with the *Contacts* table, we must have an entry in it. We will therefore set the **Required** field option to **Yes**.

Take note

On data entry, you will not be able to proceed to the next record until you have completed the *ContactID* field of the record you are entering.

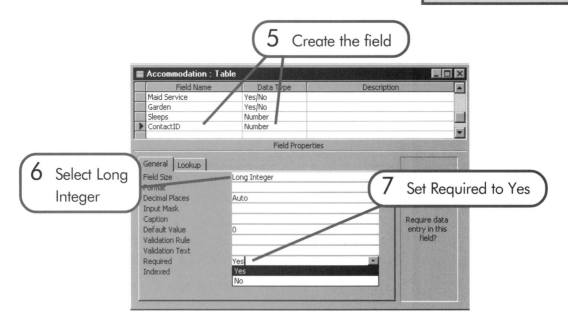

5 Create the field

6 Select Long Integer

7 Set Required to Yes

Basic steps

1 Key in the Field Name.

2 Set the Data Type to Memo or OLE Object.

3 Type in a Description if required.

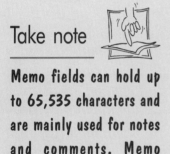

Take note

Memo fields can hold up to 65,535 characters and are mainly used for notes and comments. Memo fields cannot be indexed.

Take note

An OLE Object can be up to 1 gigabyte in size.

Memo and OLE Object

Memo

Memo fields are used to add descriptive detail to your records. You can add 'unstructured' notes in a Memo field. You can't sort or search on this field type, but it's very useful for holding additional information that you feel is relevant. Any detail specific to the property, but not covered in the other fields could be included here, e.g. distance to the nearest pub, shop, etc.

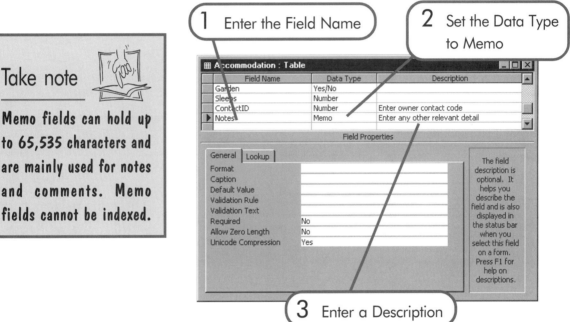

OLE Object data type

OLE stands for Object Linking and Embedding. An OLE Object is one that is created in another application that uses the OLE protocol, and is either linked to or embedded into your Access table. It may be a Word document, Excel spreadsheet, picture, sound or other binary data. In our *Accommodation* table, we could set up a field that will contain a photograph of the property we have to let.

Hyperlink

In our *Accommodation* table, we will set up a Hyperlink field that will access Word documents describing the surrounding area, main attractions, etc. for each property.

The data would be keyed in once – to a Word document. The Hyperlink field in our Access table would then link through to the document (several records can hyperlink to the same document if necessary).

Using this method general background information can be stored centrally, and shared by the records.

1 Key in the Field Name.

2 Set the Data Type to Hyperlink.

3 Type in a Description if required.

The *Accommodation* table is now complete. Save it and close the Design window.

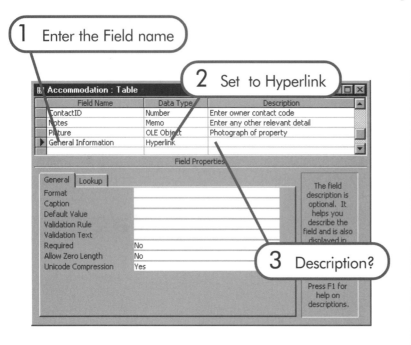

1 Enter the Field name

2 Set to Hyperlink

3 Description?

Accommodation : Table

Field Name	Data Type	Description
ContactID	Number	Enter owner contact code
Notes	Memo	Enter any other relevant detail
Picture	OLE Object	Photograph of property
General Information	Hyperlink	

Field Properties

General | Lookup

Format
Caption
Default Value
Validation Rule
Validation Text
Required — No
Allow Zero Length — No
Unicode Compression — Yes

The field description is optional. It helps you describe the field and is also displayed in

Press F1 for help on descriptions.

Take note

A Hyperlink field can store a UNC (Universal Naming Convention) path – the standard format for paths that include a LAN file server, or a URL (Uniform Resource Locator) – an address to an object, document, page or other destination on the Internet or on an intranet.

Basic steps

1 Set up the *Price Range* field – see the table. Make this field the Primary Key.

2 [Tab] to the next row.

3 Key in the Field Name e.g. *Jan–Feb*.

4 Set the Data Type to Currency.

5 [Tab] through to the next row.

6 Set up the remaining fields in this way, naming them *Mar–Apr, May–Jun, Jul–Aug, Sept–Oct, Nov–Dec.*

7 Save the Table Design naming it *Price*.

8 Close the Design window and return to the Database window.

Take note

A Currency field displays values preceded by a £ sign and with 2 decimal places, e.g. £10,750.25.

Currency

Create a new table (see page 26), then move to the Table Design window and define the first field.

Most of the fields in this table will hold monetary values, and should therefore have the Currency data type.

Price table

We'll set up the structure for the *Price* table next. Its fields, data types and properties are shown below.

Field name	Data type	Size	Other properties
Price Range	Text	1	Primary Key **Validation Rule** =”A” or =”B” or =”C” or = “D” or =”E”
Jan–Feb	Currency		
Mar–Apr	Currency		
etc			

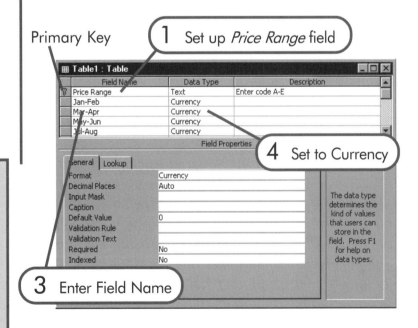

Primary Key

1 Set up *Price Range* field

4 Set to Currency

3 Enter Field Name

Summary

❑ To open a database, click the Open tool on the Database toolbar and complete the dialog box as required.

❑ AutoNumber, Date/Time, Lookup, Yes/No, Memo, OLE Object, Hyperlink and Currency data types are introduced in this chapter.

❑ For each Data Type, you can set various Field Properties as required.

❑ Use an Input Mask to control the pattern of data entered into a field.

❑ Index fields to speed up sort and search operations.

❑ If a field will have a specific value for most of the entries, set it as a default value in the property options.

❑ For fields that must have data entered, set the Required property to Yes.

❑ Validation rules can be set to help ensure the accuracy of data on input.

5 Relationships

Relationships

Now that all the tables have been set up, we can establish the relationships between the tables. Once the relationships have been established you will be able to bring together information from several tables into queries, forms and reports.

At this stage we want to set three relationships:

- one between the *Accommodation* and the *Price* tables (related through the *Price Range* field);

- between the *Accommodation* and *Type of Accommodation* tables (related through the *AccCode* field);

- between the *Contacts* and *Accommodation* tables (related through the *ContactID* field).

Relationships can be created, edited and deleted in the Relationships window.

- You must close all tables and return to the Database window before you can open the Relationships window.

Show table · Show direct relationships

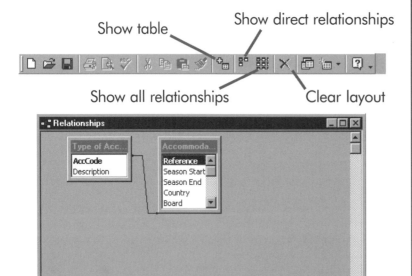

Show all relationships · Clear layout

1 From the Database window, click the Relationships tool .

or

2 Choose Relationships... from the Tools menu.

❑ The Relationships window is displayed.

Take note

If you have set up all four tables from earlier chapters, the *Accommodation* and *Type of Accommodation* tables will be displayed in the Relationships window (Access made the relationship when you set up your Lookup field in the *Accommodation* table).

If you have no related tables set up, the Show Table dialog box displays automatically when you open the Relationships window.

Basic steps

1 If necessary, click the Show Table tool to display the Show Table dialog box.

2 Select the tables that you wish to add to the Relationships window - *Price* and *Contacts* in this example.

3 Click [Add] to add them to the Relationships window.

❑ If you add a table by mistake, select it and press the [Delete] key.

4 Click [Close] on the Show Table dialog box.

The tables that you wish to create relationships between must be displayed in the Relationships window. You can add tables and queries to the Relationships window from the Show Table dialog box.

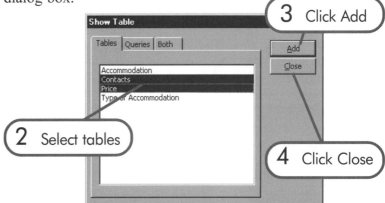

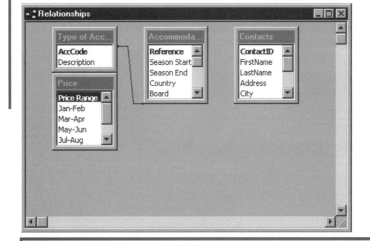

Take note

To add several tables at the same time, click on the first, hold **[Ctrl]** down and click on the others, then click **Add.**

Take note

You can easily display the design of any table from the Relationships window — you simply right-click on the table and choose **Table Design.** When you close Design View, you are returned to the Relationships window.

Making relationships

You must now make the relationships between the tables. A relationship will normally be between the Primary key field in one table and a *foreign key* field (one that refers to the primary key of a different table) in another. In our example *Price Range*, the primary key of the *Price* table, is related to *Price Range*, a foreign key field, in the *Accommodation* table.

1 Display the fields

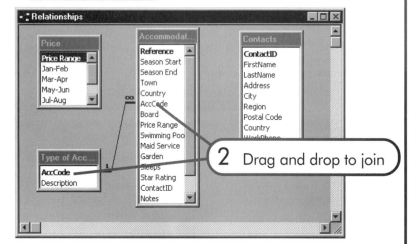

2 Drag and drop to join

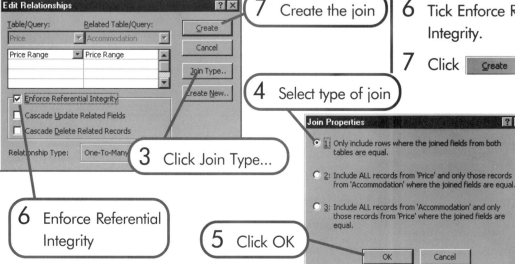

Basic steps

1 In the Relationships window, scroll through the list for each table to display the fields that are to be related, e.g. *Price Range.*

2 Drag the field name from one table onto the related field in the other.

3 At the Edit Relationships dialog box, click ⬛ Join Type.. ⬛.

4 At the Join Properties dialog box, choose the type of join required.

5 Click ⬛ OK ⬛ to return to the Edit Relationships dialog box.

6 Tick Enforce Referential Integrity.

7 Click ⬛ Create ⬛.

Referential integrity

These are the rules that are followed to preserve the defined relationships between tables when you enter or delete records.

If you enforce referential integrity, Access prevents you from:

- adding records to a related table when there is no associated record in the primary table;

- changing values in the primary table that would result in orphan (unconnected) records in a related table;

- deleting records from the primary table when there are matching related records in a related table.

Join types

- **One-to-Many** – the most common type of relationship. In these, a record in the *Price* table can have many matching records in *Accommodation*, but a record in *Accommodation* has only one matching record in *Price*.

- **One-to-One** - each record in the first table can have only one matching record in the second, and vice versa. One-to-one relationships are sometimes used to divide a table that has many fields, or to isolate some fields for security reasons. This type of relationship is not very common.

- **Many to Many** – a record in the first table can have several matching records in the second, and a record in the second can have several matching records in the first. This type of relationship is only possible by defining a third table (called a junction table) whose primary key consists of two fields – the foreign keys from both the first and second tables. A many-to-many relationship is really two one-to-many relationships with a third table.

Editing and deleting

You can edit and/or delete relationships in the Relationship window.

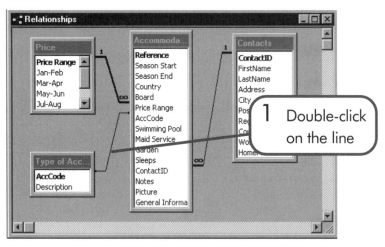

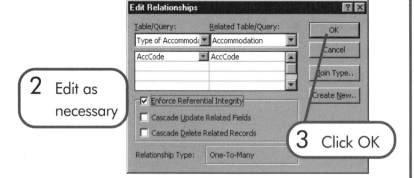

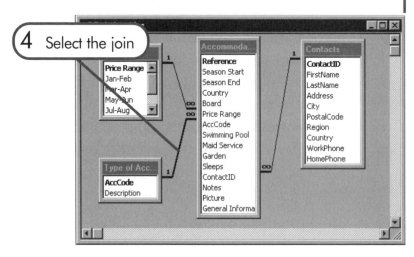

❑ To edit a relationship

1 Double-click on the Join line connecting the tables.

2 Make the alterations in the Edit Relationship dialog box.

3 Click ▭ OK ▭.

❑ To delete a relationship

4 Click the Join line.

5 Press the [Delete] key and click Yes to confirm at the prompt.

❑ Ensure that all your tables are related as required

❑ Save the relationship layout – click 🖫 and then Close.

Take note

If you have deleted a relationship that you need, *create* it again.

Basic steps

1 Display the Relationships window.

2 Open the File menu and choose Print Relationships.

3 A preview of the printout will appear. Click 🖨 on the Print Preview toolbar to print.

4 Click ⊠ to close the Preview window.

5 If you wish to save the report, click Yes at the prompt.

6 Accept or edit the report name.

7 Click [OK]. It will be listed under *Reports* in the Database window.

Printing

You can easily take a printout of the relationships between your tables for reference purposes.

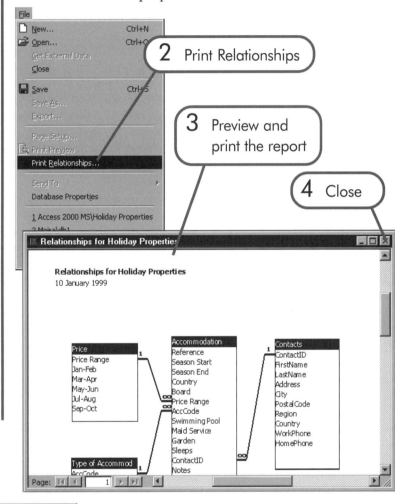

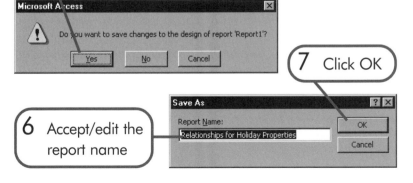

Take note

Reports are discussed in more detail in Chapter 10.

Summary

- ❑ Most tables within your database will be related to at least one other table.

- ❑ Click the Relationships tool on the Database toolbar to open the Relationships window.

- ❑ A relationship normally exists between the primary key field in one table and a foreign key field in another.

- ❑ To make a relationship, drag the related field from one table, and drop it onto the related field in another table.

- ❑ Referential integrity helps you keep related tables in sync.

- ❑ Double click a join line to edit a relationship.

- ❑ To delete a relationship, select the join line and press [Delete] on your keyboard.

- ❑ A printed report of the relationships can be useful for reference purposes.

6 Data entry and edit

Using Datasheet View

Opening a table

Once you have set up the structure of your table and set the relationships, the next stage is data entry. The table must be open for this and it should be displayed in **Datasheet** View (rather than Design View). In this view, each column of the table is a field and each row is a record. Start with the *Type of Accommodation* table, then complete the other three.

Entering data

Type the data required into each field.

Move from field to field in your table using:

[Tab]   to take you forward to the next field;

[Shift]-[Tab]   to take your back to the previous field.

Each record is saved when you move onto the next.

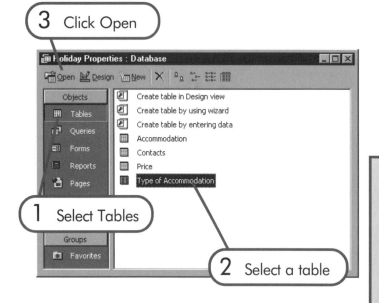

3 Click Open

1 Select Tables

2 Select a table

☐ To open a table in Datasheet View

1 Select Tables in the Objects bar in the Database window.

2 Select the table you want to open.

3 Click or double-click on the table name.

Take note

If you are working in Design View on a table, you can go directly to Datasheet View by clicking the View tool on the toolbar.

Tip

If you are using the project example, there is sample data for all four tables in the Appendix, and online at:

http://www.madesimple.co.uk

The *Reference* value is
created by AutoNumber

Input Mask   Lookup field   Default value

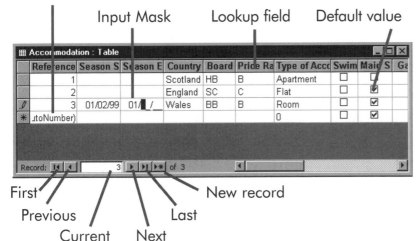

Reference	Season S	Season E	Country	Board	Price Ra	Type of Acc	Swim	Maid S	Ga
1			Scotland	HB	B	Apartment	☐	☐	
2			England	SC	C	Flat	☐	☑	
3	01/02/99	01/ /	Wales	BB	B	Room	☐	☑	
(AutoNumber)						0	☐	☑	

Record: I◀ ◀ 3 ▶ ▶I ▶* of 3

First
Previous
Current   Next
Last
New record

Take note

When entering data,
should you find an error
has been made at the
Design stage, you can go
into Design View to edit
the table design by clicking 📐.

Take note

Your entries in the
ContactID field in the
Accommodation table
need to correspond to
ContactIDs in the *Con-
tacts* table.

Inappropriate entries

If you enter incompatible data for the data type specified in a
field (e.g. if you put text in a number field, or try to key
something in that disagrees with the Input Mask for that field),
Access will display an error message. This will either be a
standard error message, or one you keyed in to the Validation
Text field at the design stage (page 50).

Microsoft Access

⚠ Enter SC, BB or HB ───── Validation Text message

OK   Help

Records in the *Type of
Accomodation* table

Current record ───

New (blank) record ───

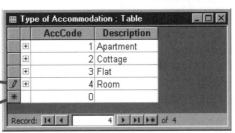

	AccCode	Description
⊞	1	Apartment
⊞	2	Cottage
⊞	3	Flat
⊞	4	Room
*	0	

Record: I◀ ◀ 4 ▶ ▶I ▶* of 4

Moving around your datasheet

In addition to using **[Tab]** and **[Shift]-[Tab]** to move between fields, there are other ways to move around:

- Point and click with the mouse to go to any field (using the scroll bars as necessary to bring the field into view).

- Use the arrows to the left of the horizontal scroll bar.

- To go to a specific record number, press **[F5],** key in the record number and press **[Enter].**

Editing

You can edit data at any time. If you move onto a field using **[Tab]** or **[Shift]-[Tab]** the data in that field is selected.

You can then:

- **Replace the current contents** – just type in the new data while the old is highlighted.

- **Edit the data** – press **[F2]** to deselect the text, then position the insertion point within the field using the **[Arrow]** keys.

- Erase the contents, by pressing **[Delete].**

Keyboard shortcuts

[PgUp]	Up a page		[Ctrl]-[PgUp]	Left a page
[↑]	Current field, previous record		[Ctrl]-[↑]	Current field, first record
[PgDn]	Down a page		[Ctrl]-[PgDn]	Right a page
[↓]	Current field, next record		[Ctrl]-[↓]	Current field, last record
[Home]	First field, current record		[Ctrl]-[Home]	First field, first record
[End]	Last field, current record		[Ctrl]-[End]	Last field, last record

Basic steps

1 Tab along to the *Type of Accommodation* field.

2 Click the drop-down arrow to display the list of options.

3 Select the one required.

The Lookup field

Notice the *Type of Accommodation* lookup field in the *Accommodation* table – it is a combo box, where you drop down the list of alternatives and select the one required. A combo box can make it simpler and quicker to enter data, and also ensures the exact wording or spelling, which may be important for searches.

(1 Move to the field)   (2 Click the drop-down arrow)

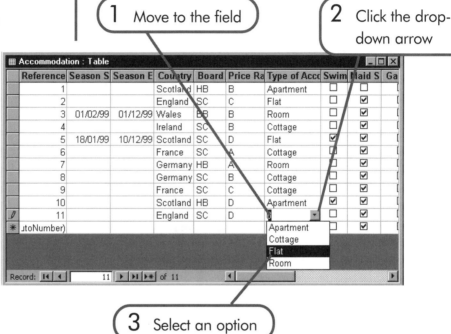

Reference	Season S	Season E	Country	Board	Price Ra	Type of Acco	Swim	Maid S	Ga
1			Scotland	HB	B	Apartment	☐	☐	
2			England	SC	C	Flat	☐	☑	
3	01/02/99	01/12/99	Wales	BB	B	Room	☐	☑	
4			Ireland	SC	B	Cottage	☐	☑	
5	18/01/99	10/12/99	Scotland	SC	D	Flat	☑	☑	
6			France	SC	A	Cottage	☐	☑	
7			Germany	HB	A	Room	☐	☑	
8			Germany	SC	B	Cottage	☐	☑	
9			France	SC	C	Cottage	☐	☑	
10			Scotland	HB	D	Apartment	☑	☑	
11			England	SC	D		☐	☑	
(AutoNumber)						Apartment	☐	☑	
						Cottage			
						Flat			
						Room			

Record: |◄ ◄ | 11 | ► ►| ►* | of 11

(3 Select an option)

Take note

We could have specified the Lookup data type for some of the other fields in our *Accommodation* table e.g. *Board, Price Range, Contact* and *Country*. It is a useful data type for fields that have a limited number of possible input options.

Pictures as OLE Objects

If you wish to insert a picture in the OLE Object field in the *Accommodation* table you can use some of the pictures in the Clip Gallery to practise with.

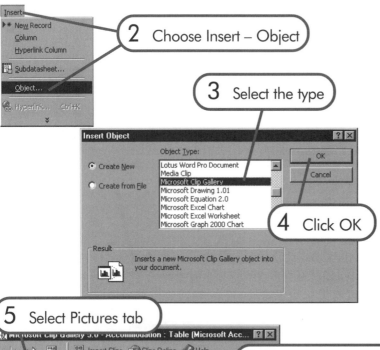

2 Choose Insert – Object

3 Select the type

4 Click OK

5 Select Pictures tab

6 Choose a category

7 Choose a picture

8 Click OK

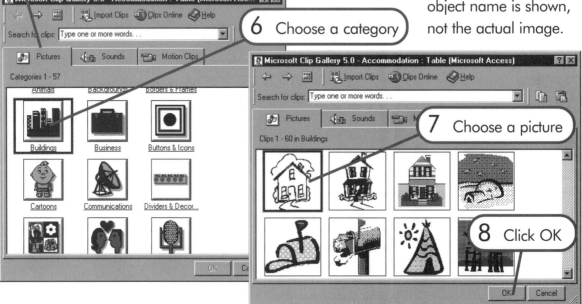

Basic steps

1 Tab along to the *Picture* field.

2 Choose Object from the Insert menu.

3 Select the Object Type – in this example Microsoft Clip Gallery.

4 Click **OK**.

5 Select the tab required – Pictures.

6 Select a picture category.

7 Choose a picture.

8 Click **OK**.

❑ In Datasheet View, the object name is shown, not the actual image.

Hyperlinks to documents

1 Tab along to the Hyperlink field.

2 Click the Insert Hyperlink tool 📷.

3 Enter the path to your document.

Or

4 Click ▮ File... ▮ and locate the document required.

5 Click ▮ OK ▮.

Additional data, e.g. general information about the locations of the properties, can be held in a set of Word documents – use any Word document to try this out.

These documents can be linked to the table through a Hyperlink in the Hyperlink field we set up (see page 56).

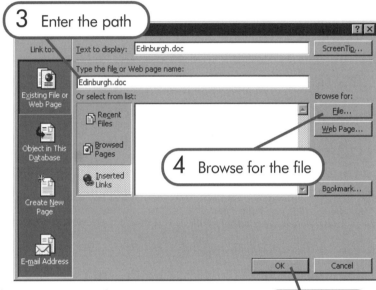

3 Enter the path

4 Browse for the file

5 Click OK

Take note

To view the document named in your Hyperlink field, click on the name, e.g. Edinburgh.doc. To return to Access from the document, click the Back tool ⇦ on the Web toolbar.

The source, not the picture, is displayed in Datasheet View

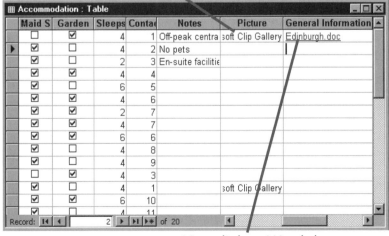

Maid S	Garden	Sleeps	Conta	Notes	Picture	General Information
☐	☑	4	1	Off-peak centra	soft Clip Gallery	Edinburgh.doc
☑	☐	4	2	No pets		
☑	☐	2	3	En-suite facilitie		
☑	☑	4	4			
☑	☐	6	5			
☑	☑	4	6			
☑	☑	2	7			
☑	☑	4	7			
☑	☑	6	6			
☑	☐	4	8			
☑	☐	4	9			
☐	☑	4	3			
☑	☐	4	1		soft Clip Gallery	
☑	☑	6	10			
☑	☐	4	11			

Record: 14 ◀ 2 ▶ ▶I ▶* of 20

Hyperlink to Word document

Adding and deleting records

Adding new records

When adding new records to your table, you add them to the end of the list of existing records. If you do not really want them at the end of the list, you will soon find out that it is very easy to sort the records into the order you want (rather than leaving them in input order).

1 Click the New Record tool ▸* or button ▸*.

2 You are moved to the first field of the first empty row under the existing records.

3 Key in the new record(s).

4 Close the datasheet or continue editing as required.

4 Close?

2 New record row

3 Enter detail

1 Click New Record

The table shown in the image:

Reference	Season S	Season E	Country	Board	Price Ra	Type of Acc	Swim
8			Germany	SC	B	Cottage	☐
9			France	SC	C	Cottage	☐
10			Scotland	HB	D	Apartment	☑
11			England	SC	D	Flat	☑
12			Wales	BB	E	Apartment	☑
			Scotland	SC	E	Flat	☐
			Italy	SC	C	Cottage	☑
			Spain	SC	D	Apartment	☑
16			England	SC	C	Cottage	☐
17			France	BB	C	Room	☐
18			Scotland	SC	B	Cottage	☐
19			Jersey	SC	C	Apartment	☑
20			Ireland	HB	D	Room	☑
(AutoNu						0	☐

Record: 21 of 21

Take note

If you are working through the project, enter the data into the *Type of Accommodation* table **before** you enter the data into the *Accommodation* table. The *Accommodation* table will lookup the *Type of Accommodation* table for the data held within it.

Basic steps

1 Click in the row selector area to select the record you no longer require.

2 Press [Delete] or click the Delete record tool .

3 At the Delete record prompt click Yes if you are sure. The record is then deleted.

Deleting records

When some of your records become redundant, you will want to delete them. Be careful when deleting records – make sure you are really finished with them first!

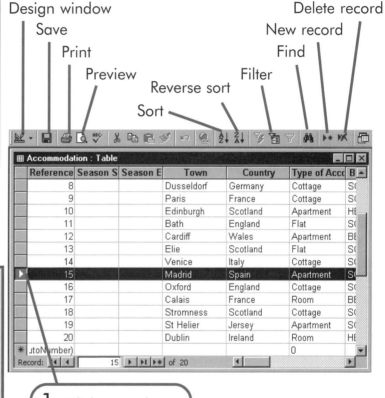

Design window
Save
Print
Preview
Sort
Reverse sort
Filter
Find
New record
Delete record

Reference	Season S	Season E	Town	Country	Type of Accc	B
8			Dusseldorf	Germany	Cottage	SC
9			Paris	France	Cottage	SC
10			Edinburgh	Scotland	Apartment	HE
11			Bath	England	Flat	SC
12			Cardiff	Wales	Apartment	BE
13			Elie	Scotland	Flat	SC
14			Venice	Italy	Cottage	SC
15			Madrid	Spain	Apartment	SC
16			Oxford	England	Cottage	SC
17			Calais	France	Room	BE
18			Stromness	Scotland	Cottage	SC
19			St Helier	Jersey	Apartment	SC
20			Dublin	Ireland	Room	HE
* utoNumber)					0	

Record: 15 of 20

1 Click row selector

2 Press [Delete]

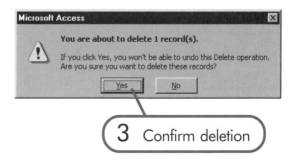

Microsoft Access

⚠ You are about to delete 1 record(s).

If you click Yes, you won't be able to undo this Delete operation. Are you sure you want to delete these records?

Yes   No

3 Confirm deletion

Take note

To select several adjacent records, click and drag in the row selector area until you have highlighted all the records you want to delete.

Using Form View

As an alternative to working in Datasheet View, you could let Access create a basic form for you using AutoForm.

AutoForm will take the fields, and arrange them in a simple list layout that displays one record at a time. (If there are lots of fields in each record you may have to scroll through the form to view them all.) The table name will be displayed at the top of each record.

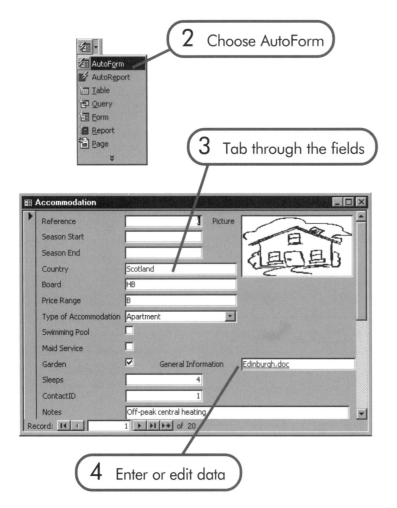

2 Choose AutoForm

3 Tab through the fields

4 Enter or edit data

Basic steps

1 At the Database window select the table.

2 Pick AutoForm from the New Object list.

❑ A simple form is displayed on the screen

3 Use [Tab] or [Shift]-[Tab] to move between fields (or point and click with the mouse).

4 At each field, key in the required data.

5 When you reach the last field, pressing [Tab] takes you to the first field in the next record.

Take note

In the illustration, the OLE Object field and Hyperlink field have been moved so that you can see the complete form on the screen at the one time. You will see how to move elements on page 116.

Basic steps

1 Click the Save tool .

or

2 If you have closed the form without saving, click `Yes` at the prompt.

3 At the Save As dialog box enter a name, e.g. *Accommodation Simple Form.*

4 Click `OK`.

❑ The form will be listed on the Forms area of the Database window.

Naming your form

When you have keyed in all the data, you will want to return to your Database window.

Save and name the form before you go. You will be prompted to do this if you try to close without saving.

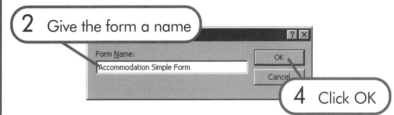

2 Give the form a name

4 Click OK

The Form is listed in the Database window

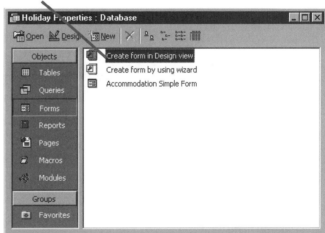

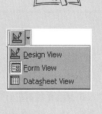

Adding a field

New fields can easily be added to an existing table. Try adding two fields to the *Accommodation* table.

● *Town* has the Text data type, and will fit above *Country*;

● *Star Rating* will go above *ContactID*. This field should have the Number data type and an Integer format. Add a Validation Rule set to accept only a 1 or 2 or 3 or 4 (our star rating system).

● If you are working through the project make up some *Town* and *Star Rating* details.

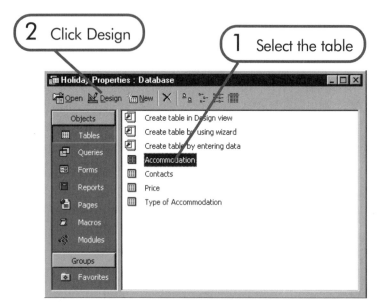

2 Click Design

1 Select the table

Take note

To add a field at the end of your field list, simply scroll down to the first empty row, and key in the details required.

1 At the Database window, select the table whose design you want to edit.

2 Click ▟ Design .

3 Select the row (field) that you want to have below the new one.

4 Click the Insert Rows tool ∃←. A new field is added above the selected one.

5 Define the field name, data type, description, and field properties.

6 Add other fields as required.

7 Save the changes – click the Save tool ▣ .

8 Respond to the Data Integrity Rules prompt.

9 Close the Design window by clicking its Close button.

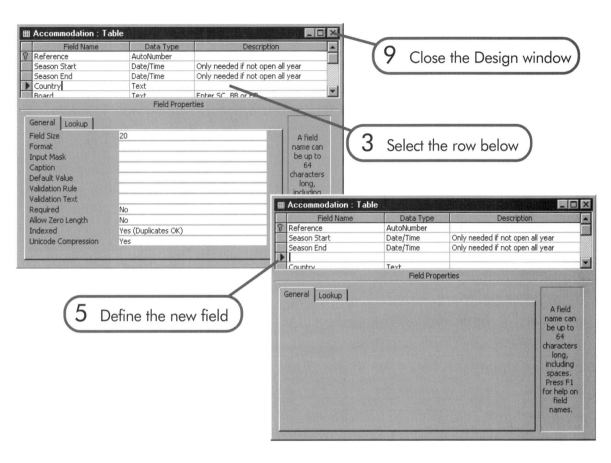

9 Close the Design window

3 Select the row below

5 Define the new field

Take note

If you add Validation Rules (see page 50) to a new field, this prompt appears when you try to save the new design.

With a new field, which contains no data, click No . If you have changed the properties of an existing field (with data in it) click Yes to check the data against the new rules or No to leave it unchecked.

Microsoft Access

⚠ Data integrity rules have been changed; existing data may not be valid for the new rules.

This process may take a long time. Do you want the existing data to be tested with the new rules?

Yes   No   Cancel

79

Deleting a field

Redundant fields are just as easily removed. Any data held within a field that you delete is permanently erased – so be careful with this one!

● Before deleting a field, go into Datasheet View and check the field contents. If all the data in the field is redundant, you could remove the field.

Basic steps

1 Open the table in Design View.

2 Select the row (field) you want to delete.

3 Click the Delete Rows tool ⧉.

4 Confirm the deletion at the prompt.

5 If an Index will also be deleted, you will be prompted to confirm the deletion again.

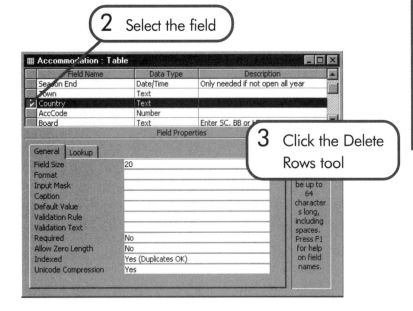

2 Select the field

3 Click the Delete Rows tool

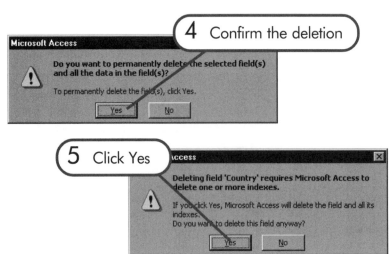

4 Confirm the deletion

5 Click Yes

Tip

If you delete a field or change its properties, then change your mind, close the table without saving the changes. When you reopen it, the field (and its contents) will still be there.

Changing field properties

1 Open the table in Design View.

2 Select a Currency field.

3 Press [F6] to move to the lower pane.

4 Open the Decimal Places list and change the property to 0.

5 Repeat for all fields.

❑ Moving fields

6 In Design View, click in the selector bar.

7 With the pointer in the selector bar area, drag and drop the field into its new position.

8 Save the changes and close the window.

Field properties can also be modified as required. In the *Price* table, we can change the field properties of the fields with a **Currency** data type to show 0 decimal places.

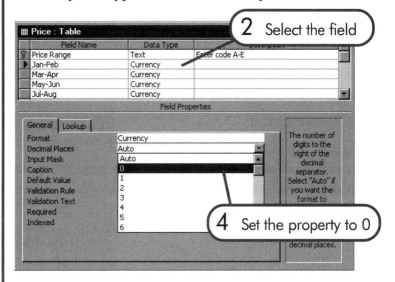

Moving fields

You can change the order of your fields in either Design or Datasheet View.

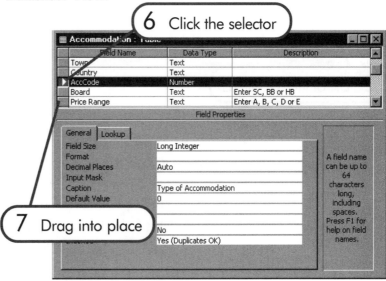

Take note

In Datasheet View, you can move a field by dragging the field name at the top of the column.

Primary key and indexes

You may decide that the field that you originally set as your Primary Key is no longer appropriate.

- Changing the primary key is simply a case of setting a new one (see page 29);

- Removing the primary key without setting a new one is also very easy. The primary key tool is a toggle – it switches the status on and off. Select the field that currently has primary key status and click the Primary Key tool. (Set your primary key again if necessary.)

You can display a list of the fields that you have indexed in your table. This gives you a quick check on what has and hasn't been indexed.

Changing the primary key is simply a case of setting a new one (see page 29)

1 In Design View, click the Indexes tool .

2 A list of the indexed fields is displayed.

3 Click the Indexes tool again to close the dialog box (or click its Close button).

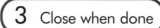

3 Close when done

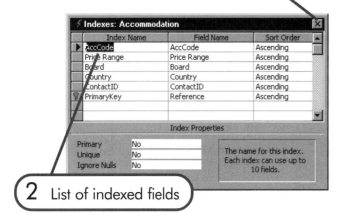

2 List of indexed fields

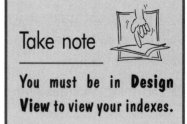

Take note

You must be in **Design View** to view your indexes.

Take note

Viewing the Indexes dialog box can be useful to let you check what fields have and have not been indexed – it's a lot quicker then checking each field individually in Design View.

Basic steps

1 Open the *Accommodation* table in Design View.

2 Move to the *Town* field.

3 Press [F6] to go to the lower pane.

4 Set the *Indexed* field to Yes (Duplicates OK) as we may have several properties in one town.

5 Do the same with the *Star Rating* field.

6 Save the changes, and close the table.

Tip

To see a list of the Indexed fields in your table, open the Indexes dialog box from Design View — click the Indexes tool. You can edit the properties of any entry — i.e. Index Name, Sort Order, Primary key status, etc. — from this dialog box.

Adjusting indexes

Fields can be indexed at the initial design stage, or during a later edit of the design.

Index those fields you will want to sort on or search on, as it speeds up sorting and searching. In the *Accommodation* table, we could index the *Town* and *Star Rating* fields, as we would probably want to sort or search on those fields, e.g. to sort accommodation into town order, or to search for accommodation in certain towns or with specific star ratings.

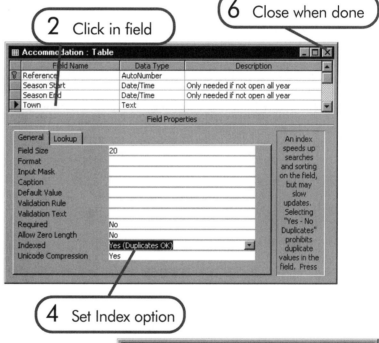

New list of indexed fields

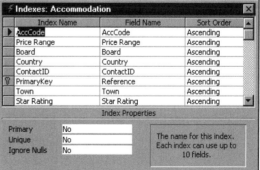

Summary

- ❑ To add or edit date, open the table in Datasheet View.

- ❑ To move between fields use [Tab] or [Shift]-[Tab].

- ❑ To move between records use the arrows on the left of the status bar, or the scroll bars and the mouse.

- ❑ To go to a specific record press [F5], key in the record number and press [Enter].

- ❑ The contents of a field can be edited, replaced or deleted during initial data entry or at any later time.

- ❑ A drop-down list displays the options available in a Lookup field.

- ❑ Use Autoform to display records in a form layout.

- ❑ You can insert pictures into records as OLE objects, or Hyperlink documents.

- ❑ To add a record to your table, click the New Record tool on the toolbar, then key in the detail.

- ❑ To delete a record, select it, then press [Delete].

- ❑ You can add a field anywhere in a table.

- ❑ When deleting a field, make sure that it is the right one and you really don't want it!

- ❑ Field Properties are easily changed if necessary.

- ❑ The order or fields can be rearranged in either Design or Datasheet View.

- ❑ The the primary key can be changed or removed.

- ❑ Fields that are likely to be sorted or searched on should be indexed.

- ❑ Remember to save your edited Design.

Take note

If you are working through the project in this book, add the data in the Appendix to all four tables before continuing.

7 Datasheet display

Fonts

The default character style (font) is Arial, 10 point. You may want to change the font style or size if you are formatting your datasheet with a view to printing it. You might want to use a larger font, or make the print bold, for example.

You can change the font style and/or size by using the **Font** dialog box.

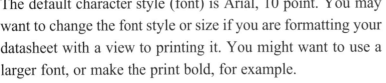

1 Choose Format – Font...

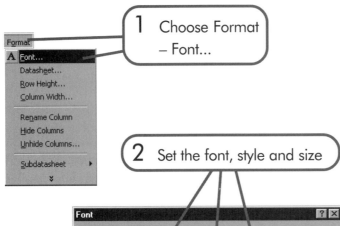

2 Set the font, style and size

3 Click OK

Check the appearance in the Sample box

Basic steps

1 Choose Font... from the Format menu.

2 In the Font dialog box, select the font, size and style.

❑ The Sample area shows the effect your selections will have on the characters.

3 Click OK to return to the datasheet with your new settings.

Take note

When you change the font attributes, they are changed for the whole datasheet, not just the column(s) or row(s) you have selected.

Basic steps

1 Open the Format menu.
2 Click Datasheet...
3 Complete the Datasheet Formatting dialog box as required.
4 Click OK.

There are several other datasheet formatting options that you can change.

You can print data from your table in Datasheet View, so you might want to consider customising the datasheet before you print (see pages 92 and 93).

By default, gridlines are displayed between the rows and columns on your table. Most of the time this is what you want, but, particularly if you are going to print your table in Datasheet View, you might prefer to switch them off. Gridlines can be switched on and off in the Datasheet Formatting dialog box.

Take note

If you make the Gridline colour the same as the background colour, your gridlines are 'hidden'.

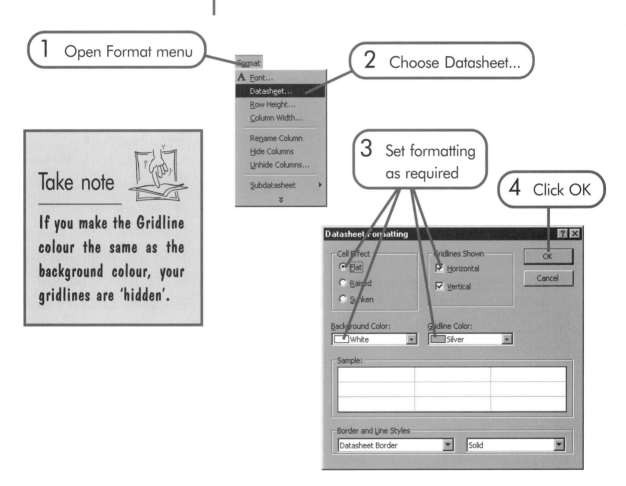

1 Open Format menu

2 Choose Datasheet...

3 Set formatting as required

4 Click OK

Hiding columns

There may be times when you do not want all the columns in your table to be visible. You may be concentrating on a task that only uses certain fields and decide to hide the ones that are of no concern at the moment, or you might want to print out only certain columns from your datasheet.

1 Select one column by clicking in the Field Name row.

or

Select a set of adjacent columns by dragging along the field name row.

2 Choose Hide Columns from the Format menu.

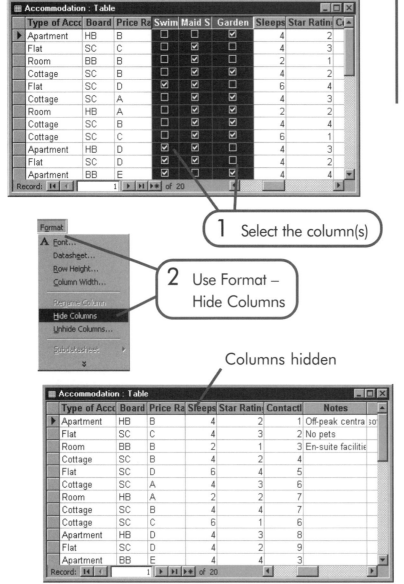

1 Select the column(s)

2 Use Format – Hide Columns

Columns hidden

Take note

You can also hide columns by dragging the vertical line between the field names left, until the field to the left of the line disappears. Columns that appear hidden this way may register 'showing' in the Show Columns dialog box. You must hide the column completely to give it 'hidden' status.

88

Basic steps

1 Open the Format menu and choose Unhide Columns.

❑ The Unhide columns dialog box appears. The columns currently showing have a tick beside them.

2 Scroll up and down the list to locate the field name you want if necessary.

3 Toggle the Show/Hide status by selecting the fields you wish to show, or deselecting those you wish to hide.

4 When you have speci-fied what fields to show, and which to hide, click Close.

Showing columns

If you have hidden some columns, there will come a time when you need to show them again. The easiest way to reveal hidden columns is to use the Unhide Columns command in the Format menu.

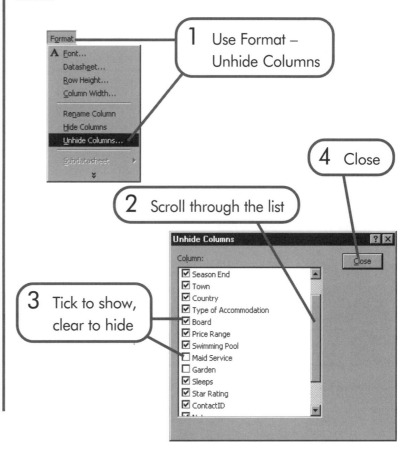

1 Use Format – Unhide Columns

2 Scroll through the list

3 Tick to show, clear to hide

4 Close

Take note

You can 'show' hidden columns using the click and drag method, but it can be tricky! Locating the column border in the field name row (where one border overlays another when columns are hidden) can be a frustrating exercise using the mouse!

89

Freezing columns

Basic steps

There will be times that you need to view columns, which are distant from each other in your table, on the screen at the same time. This can be done by hiding (see page 88) or by **freezing** columns at the left side of your table. They will remain in position while the other columns can be scrolled in and out of sight. If gridlines are not displayed, a thick line appears to the right of the frozen columns.

1 Select the column(s).

2 Choose Freeze Columns from the Format menu.

3 The column(s) are moved, if necessary, and frozen at the left of the table.

❑ To unfreeze columns

4 Choose Unfreeze All Columns from the Format menu.

1 Select the column(s)

		Contact ID	First Name	Last Name	Address	City	Regi
▶	⊞	1	John	Johnston	24 Main Street	INVERNESS	Highland
	⊞	2	Elaine	Anderson	22 St Stephen Street	EDINBURGH	Midlothia
	⊞	3	Elizabeth	Watson	14 Mill Wynd West	GLASGOW	Strathcly
	⊞	4	Gordon	McPherson	14 Worthington Way	BIRMIGHAM	Mildands
	⊞	5	Hanz	Beckenbaur	24 Lang Strasse	BERLIN	
	⊞	6	Andrews	Simpson	10 Dolphin Road	LONDON	
	⊞	7	Alice	Aberley	St Stephens Manse	PETERLEE	Co Durha
	⊞	8	Brian	Allanson	328 Bath Road	ILFORD	Essex
	⊞	9	Pamela	Johnston	10 Wilson Way	DEREHAM	Norfolk
	⊞	10	Joan	Robertson	24 West Linton Way	KENDAL	Cumbria
	⊞	11	William	Flux	132 London Road	CARNO	Montgom
	⊞	12	Amanda	Wilson	14 High Way	LAMPETER	Dyfed
	⊞	13	William	Robertson	Hill View Rise	STROMNESS	Orkney
	⊞	14	Suzanne	Young	24 Causeway St	CLEMENT	Jersey
	⊞	15	Paul	Mitchell	45 Hill Top View	ABERDEEN	Aberdeer

Record: 14 ◀ 1 ▶ ▶I ▶* of 15

2 Use Format – Freeze Columns

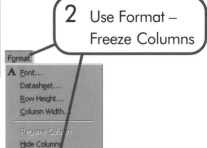

Format
A Font...
Datasheet...
Row Height...
Column Width...
Rename Column
Hide Columns
Unhide Columns...
Freeze Columns
Unfreeze All Columns
Subdatasheet ▶

3 Columns frozen

		Contact ID	First Name	Last Name	Work Phone	Home Phone	
	⊞	1	John	Johnston	01463 2210	01463 1010	
	⊞	2	Elaine	Anderson	0131 442 1021	0131 556 0212	
	⊞	3	Elizabeth	Watson	0131 665 1043	0141 510 5103	
	⊞	4	Gordon	McPherson	0121 557 9321	0121 676 1999	
	⊞	5	Hanz	Beckenbaur	00 49 30 121	00 49 30 435	
	⊞	6	Andrews	Simpson	0181 475 1010	0171 442 4102	
	⊞	7	Alice	Aberley	0191 575 3928	0191 653 1843	
	⊞	8	Brian	Allanson	0181 543 6758	0171 544 1234	
	⊞	9	Pamela	Johnston	01362 331112	01362 574098	
	⊞	10	Joan	Robertson	01539 561732	01539 665577	
	⊞	11	William	Flux	01686 203956	01686 105619	
	⊞	12	Amanda	Wilson	01570 30651	01570 51234	
▶	⊞	13	William	Robertson	01856 103212	01856 114322	
	⊞	14	Suzanne	Young	01534 13261	01534 66310	
	⊞	15	Paul	Mitchell	01224 10231	01224 54123	

Record: 14 ◀ 13 ▶ ▶I ▶* of 15

The thick line marks the edge of the frozen columns

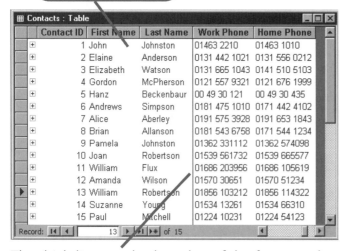

Take note

Columns that have been frozen, remain at the left edge when unfrozen.

Print Preview

1 Open the table you want to print in Datasheet View.

2 Format it as required.

3 Click the Print Preview tool ⌕.

❑ Your table is displayed in the Print Preview screen.

Take note

If you want to edit before printing, close the Print Preview and return to Datasheet View by clicking Close or ▦ on the Print Preview toolbar.

Take note

The page header contains the table name and the current date; the footer contains the page number. These can be switched on or off in Page Setup.

Now that you have some data in your table(s), you will most likely want to print it out at some stage. There are various ways of doing this, but an easy way to begin with is to print from Datasheet View.

Once the datasheet display has been formatted to your satisfaction, you can print the table.

Do a Print Preview first and check that the layout is okay on screen, before you commit it to paper.

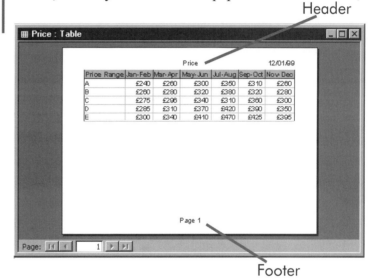

Print Preview toolbar

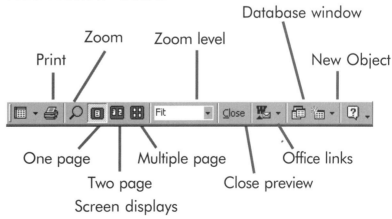

Page Setup

If you want to change the margins, paper size or orientation of your page, use the Page Setup dialog box to make the necessary changes. You can move to the Page Setup dialog box from the Print Preview screen or from Datasheet View.

Basic steps

1 Open the File menu.

2 Select Page Setup.

3 Complete the Page Setup dialog box as required.

4 Click   OK   .

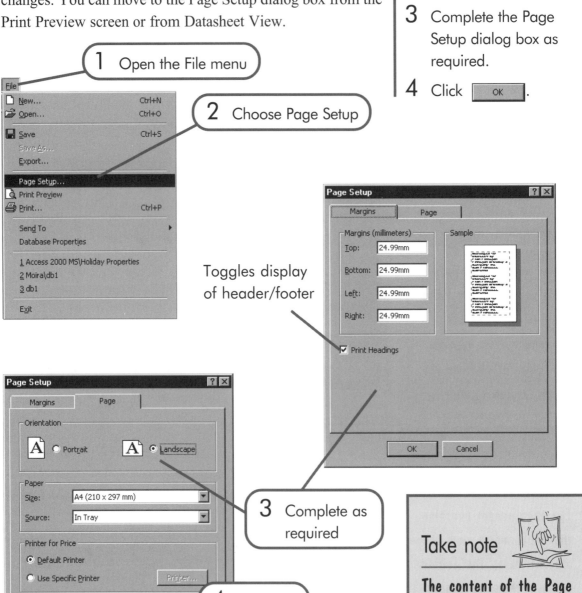

1   Open the File menu

2   Choose Page Setup

Toggles display of header/footer

3   Complete as required

4   Click OK

Take note

The content of the Page Setup dialog box varies from printer to printer.

Basic steps

1 If you want to print certain records, select them now.

C Choose Print from the File menu.

3 Complete the Print dialog box as required.

4 Click [OK].

If the table is formatted and the Page Setup is okay, you can go ahead and print your table. You can print directly from Datasheet View, or from the Print Preview screen. It does not matter whether you are in Datasheet Vview or the Print Preview screen, the routine is the same.

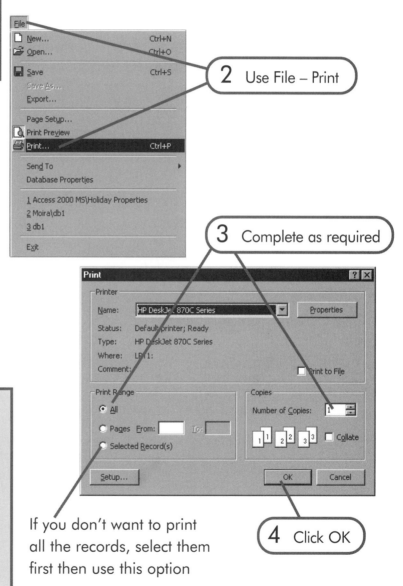

2 Use File – Print

3 Complete as required

4 Click OK

If you don't want to print all the records, select them first then use this option

Take note

To send your table directly to the printer, using the default print settings, click the Print tool 🖨.

Tip

Multiple copies are printed quicker uncollated – i.e. all page 1s then all page 2s, etc., but you will have to collate them by hand later.

Summary

- ❏ To change the font used in your datasheet, choose Format – Font and select from the options.

- ❏ The Gridlines can be changed from the Datasheet Formatting dialog box.

- ❏ To hide columns, select the columns you want to hide then choose Format – Hide Columns.

- ❏ To show hidden columns, choose Format – Unhide Columns and complete the dialog box as required.

- ❏ To stop columns scrolling off the screen, select them and choose Format – Freeze Columns.

- ❏ To unfreeze your columns, choose Format – Unfreeze All Columns.

- ❏ To preview your datasheet before printing, click the Print Preview tool on the toolbar.

- ❏ To change the margins, paper size or orientation of the paper, go into Page Setup.

- ❏ The page header and footer can be switched on/off in the Page Setup dialog box.

- ❏ To print your datasheet, click the Print tool on the Datasheet toolbar or on the Print Preview toolbar.

8 Sorting and searching

Find

With larger databases, it is impractical to locate records by scrolling through, reading each row. The **Find** command will locate records that contain a specified item of text. Find works most efficiently if you know what field the data is in (so you don't need to search the whole table), and the field is *indexed*.

● If you know what field the data is in, position the insertion point in the field in Datasheet View before you start.

Choose the **Match** option to suit the target data. It can be *Any Part of Field*, *Whole Field* or *Start of Field*.

Basic steps

1 Click the Find tool on the Datasheet toolbar.

2 Key the target data in the Find What: area.

3 In Look In: select the field if known.

4 In Match: indicate where the data appears in the field.

5 Click ☐Find Next☐ to start the search, or to look for the next match.

6 When you have found the record click ☐ Cancel ☐.

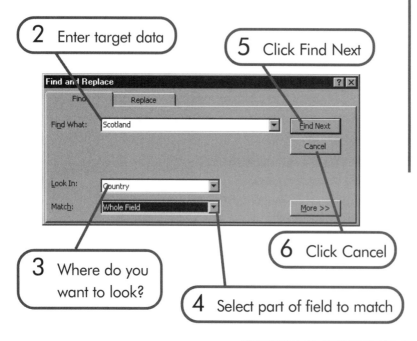

2 Enter target data

5 Click Find Next

3 Where do you want to look?

4 Select part of field to match

6 Click Cancel

Tip

When the Find and Replace dialog box appears, drag on its title bar to move it so that it does not obscure the data you are working with.

Basic steps

1 Click the Find tool and go to the Replace tab.

2 Key the target data in the Find What: area.

3 Complete the Replace with:, Look In: and Search: fields .

❑ Selective replace

4 Click [Find Next].

5 Once you find the data, click [Replace].

or

6 Click [Find Next] to move to the next occurence.

7 Click [Cancel] when you are finished.

❑ Global replacement

8 Click [Replace All].

9 Click [Yes] to confirm the replacement.

Replace

You can quickly change the contents of several fields using the Replace option.

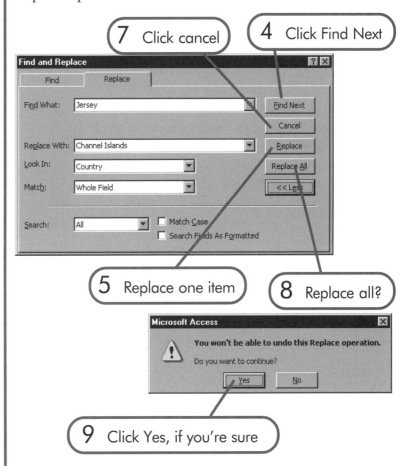

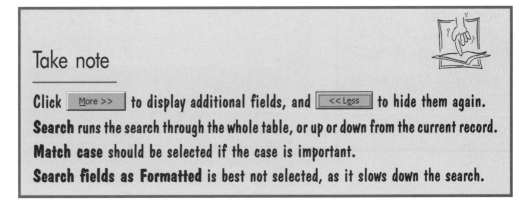

Take note

Click [More >>] to display additional fields, and [<< Less] to hide them again.

Search runs the search through the whole table, or up or down from the current record.

Match case should be selected if the case is important.

Search fields as Formatted is best not selected, as it slows down the search.

Filter By Selection

When working within a table, you might want to display a subset of the records held based on some criteria, e.g. all the properties in Scotland. You can use **Filter By Selection** techniques for this.

1   Select the criteria

You can repeat the filter process as many times as you like, to get down to the records you want.

Take note

1   Select the text you want to base your filter on, e.g. 'Scotland' in the *Country* field.

2   Click the Filter By Selection tool 🔽.

❑   Records matching the selection are displayed.

3   Repeat the process if you want a sub-set of your new list, e.g. only flats.

4   Click the Remove Filter tool 🔽 to display all your records again.

Display after first level of filtering   3   Select again?

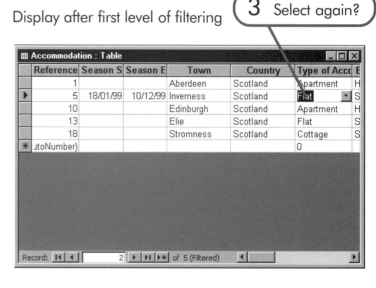

Basic steps

1 Click the Filter By Form tool 🖫.

❏ As you move from field to field, you will notice that each becomes a Combo type box, with a drop-down arrow.

2 Select the criteria required from the drop-down lists.

3 Switch to the Or tab and set options here if alternatives are wanted.

4 Click the Apply Filter tool 𝖸.

As an alternative to using Filter By Selection, you could use Filter By Form. Using Filter By Form, you can specify multiple criteria at the same time, rather than one at a time, e.g. 'England' in *Country* and 'SC' in *Board*.

You can also set alternative criteria, using the **Or** tab. If 'Scotland' in *Country* was selected here, the filter would pick up properties in either country.

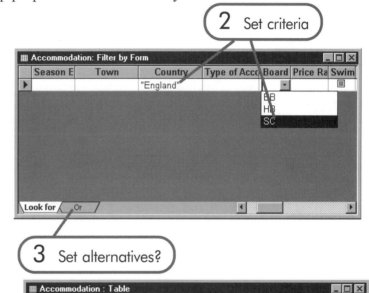

2 Set criteria

3 Set alternatives?

Self-catering in England

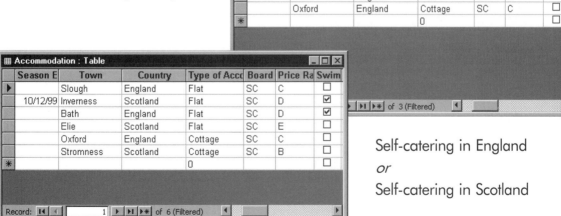

Self-catering in England
or
Self-catering in Scotland

The subdatasheet

You may have noticed that in tables whose primary key is a foreign key in another table, the left-most column in the table contains a plus sign. This indicates that there is a subdatasheet of related records that can be displayed directly from the table, e.g. *Price*, *Type of Accomodation* and *Contacts* all have links from their primary key to the *Accomodation* table.

You can easily display the related records for individual records or for all the records in the table.

1 Open a table where the records are related through the primary key to records in another table.

❑ To expand the subdatasheet

2 Click the plus sign to the left of the record .

❑ To collapse the subdatasheet

3 Click the minus sign to the left of the record you wish to collapse.

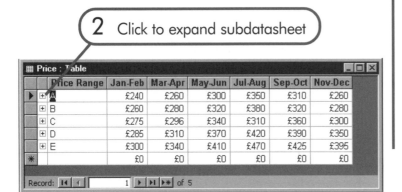

2 Click to expand subdatasheet

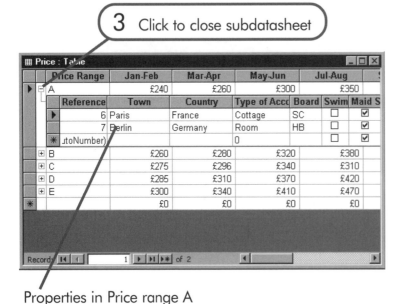

3 Click to close subdatasheet

Properties in Price range A

Take note

If you make changes to either the main data in the table or the data in the subdatasheet, you will be asked if you want to save the changes when you close the table.

100

- ❏ To expand or collapse the subdatasheet for all records

1 Open the Format menu.

2 Select Subdatasheet.

3 Choose Expand All or Collapse All as wanted.

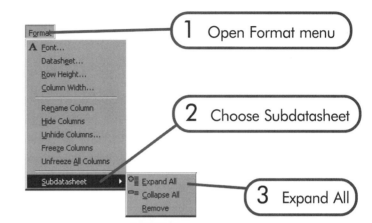

1 Open Format menu

2 Choose Subdatasheet

3 Expand All

Subdatasheets expanded for all records

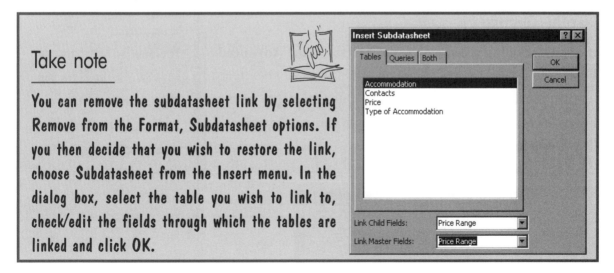

Sort

When you key records into your table, they normally appear in the order in which they were entered. There will be times when you need the records in a different order, ascending or descending, using some other field in the table. For example, in the *Accommodation* table, you might decide to rearrange, or **sort**, your records into *Country*, *Town* or *Star Rating* order.

Sorting your records on one field is very easy. We could use the *Accommodation* table to try this out.

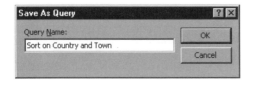

Basic steps

1 Open the table you want to sort (in our case *Accommodation*).

2 Put the insertion point anywhere in the field you want to sort your records on.

3 Click the ⌷ or ⌷ tool.

❑ The records are sorted in Ascending or Descending order, as selected.

Saving queries

If you have set up a complex set of criteria in the **Advanced Filter/Sort** grid (see opposite), you might want to save it, so you can use it again. Click the **Save As Query** tool on the **Filter/Sort** toolbar and enter a meaningful name at the Save As Query dialog box.

> ### Take note
>
> You can be anywhere, in any row, in the field you want to sort on. The whole table will be sorted in ascending or descending order on the data in that field.

Basic steps

1 Choose Filter, then Advanced Filter/Sort… from the Records menu.

2 Double-click on each field required in the fields list to add it to the grid in the lower part of the screen.

3 Select Ascending or Descending Sort order for each field from the drop-down list.

4 Click the Apply/Re-move Filter tool ▽ on the Filter/Sort toolbar.

5 The sorted table is displayed.

If you need to sort your table on more than one field, you have to set the sort up as a **Query**. You can do this by going into the **Filter** dialog box.

Multi-level sorts take longer than single field sorts, and obviously the more levels you sort to, the longer it takes.

We'll do a simple multi-level sort, rearranging the records in the *Accommodation* table by *Country*, then by *Town*.

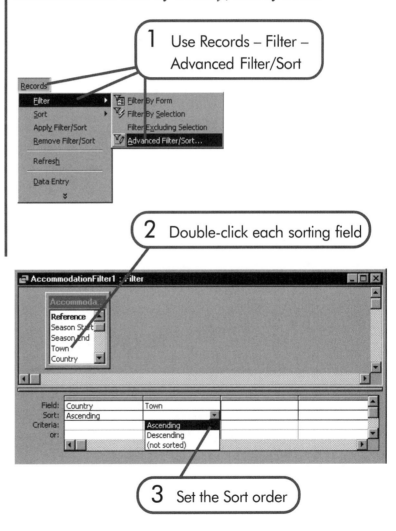

1 Use Records – Filter – Advanced Filter/Sort

2 Double-click each sorting field

3 Set the Sort order

Take note

If you need to clear existing criteria from the grid, click the Clear Grid tool ✕ then set up your new criteria.

Simple Query Wizard

Basic steps

If you have more than one table in your database, you may need to interrogate several at the same time to locate the information you require, e.g. the name and phone number of a contact, plus the town and star rating of a property. A query will extract from your tables a subset of records that meet specific criteria. The Simple Query Wizard will help you do this.

1 Select Queries in the Object bar.

2 Double-click Create query by using wizard.

or

3 Click New, choose Simple Query Wizard from the New Query dialog box and click OK.

4 Select the table or query that contains the fields you want.

5 Select the field(s) and add them to Selected fields list.

Repeat steps 4 and 5 as necessary.

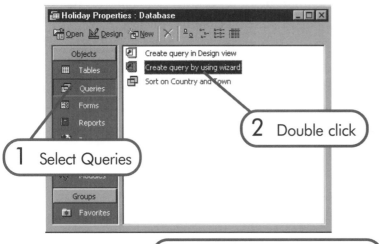

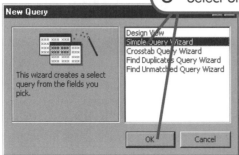

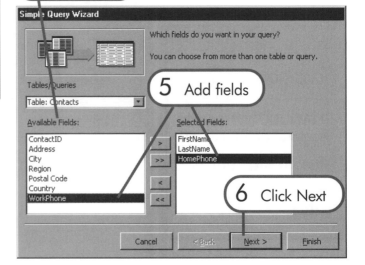

Tip

Have a look at the other wizards in the New Query dialog box.

6 Click Next.

7 Select Detail and click Next.

8 Edit the query name if necessary.

9 Select Open the query to view information.

10 Click Finish.

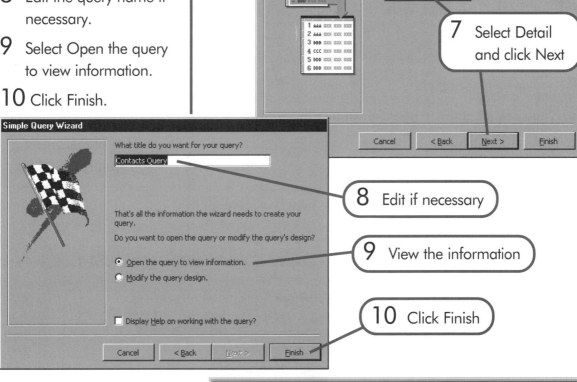

Simple Query Wizard

Would you like a detail or summary query?

● Detail (shows every field of every record)

○ Summary

Summary Options ...

7 Select Detail and click Next

Cancel | < Back | Next > | Finish

Simple Query Wizard

What title do you want for your query?

Contacts Query

That's all the information the wizard needs to create your query.

Do you want to open the query or modify the query's design?

● Open the query to view information.

○ Modify the query design.

☐ Display Help on working with the query?

Cancel | < Back | Next > | Finish

8 Edit if necessary

9 View the information

10 Click Finish

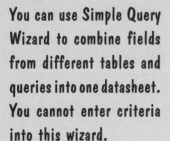

Take note

You can use Simple Query Wizard to combine fields from different tables and queries into one datasheet. You cannot enter criteria into this wizard.

Contacts Query : Select Query

First Name	Last Name	Home Phone	Town	Type of Acc	Sleeps	Star
John	Johnston	01463 1010	Aberdeen	Apartment	4	2
Pamela	Johnston	01362 574098	Bath	Flat	4	2
Alice	Aberley	0191 653 1843	Berlin	Room	2	2
Amanda	Wilson	01570 51234	Calais	Room	2	3
Elizabeth	Watson	0141 510 5103	Cardiff	Room	2	1
Elizabeth	Watson	0141 510 5103	Cardiff	Apartment	4	4
Gordon	McPherson	0121 676 1999	Cork	Cottage	4	2
Suzanne	Young	01534 66310	Dublin	Room	2	4
Alice	Aberley	0191 653 1843	Dusseldorf	Cottage	4	4
Brian	Allanson	0171 544 1234	Edinburgh	Apartment	4	3
John	Johnston	01463 1010	Elie	Flat	4	3
Hanz	Beckenbaur	00 49 30 435	Inverness	Flat	6	4
William	Flux	01686 105619	Madrid	Apartment	4	1

Record: |◄| ◄ | 1 | ► | ►| | ►* | of 20

Query combining fields from *Contacts* and *Accommodation*

105

Multi-table queries

As an alternative to using the wizard, you could set up a query in Design View to combine data from several tables or queries. In Design View, you can also specifiy the criteria that you wish to use to select the records required.

This example draws data from three tables. I want to find properties that sleep more than four people, and for each matching property, I want details of:

- what town the property is in (*Accommodation*);

- the type of property (*Accommodation*);

- the contact's name and telephone number (*Contacts*);

- the cost of the property in May/June (*Price*).

To do this in Access you set up a query from the Database window.

❑ Adding the tables

1 Select Queries in the Object bar in the Database window and click New.

2 Select Design View, and click OK.

❑ This opens the Select Query and Show Table dialog boxes, where you specify the tables you want to query and set up your criteria.

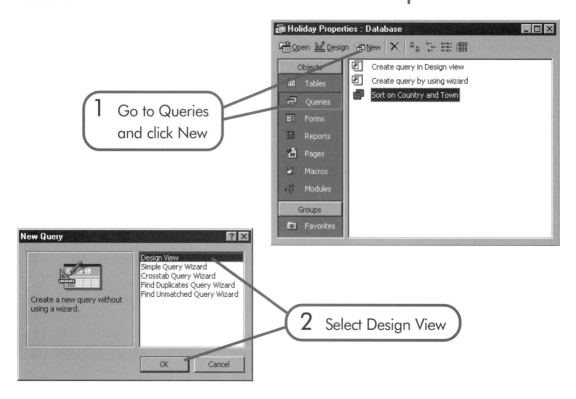

1 Go to Queries and click New

2 Select Design View

106

3 If the Show Table dialog box is not open, click the Show Table tool 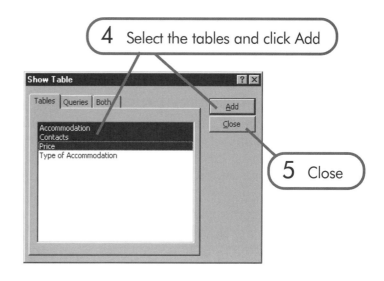.

4 Select the table(s) that you want to query and click [Add].

5 When all the necessary tables have been added, click [Close] to close the dialog box.

Join lines

In the upper half of the **Select Query** dialog box, the join lines between the tables are displayed. These lines indicate the fields that relate one table to another. Here the *Accommodation* and *Contacts* tables are related through the *ContactID* field. The *Accommodation* and *Price* tables are related through the *Price Range* field. The primary key in each table is displayed in bold type in the field list.

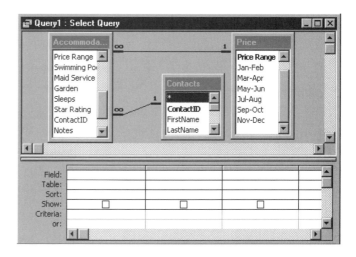

Setting the query criteria

The next stage is to select fields to be included in the output, and to specify any criteria that are to be used to select records.

We want the *Town* and *Sleeps* fields from the *Accommodation* table, with the criteria >**4** (more than 4) set for *Sleeps*; *FirstName*, *LastName* and *HomePhone* from the *Contacts* table and *May-June* from the *Price* table.

If we set **Sort** mode, we can also determine the order of records in the final output.

1 Select fields for inclusion by double-clicking on them in the field lists.

2 Set the sort and/or selection criteria (if required).

3 If you do not want to display the field contents when you run the query, clear the Show checkbox.

4 Click to save the query.

5 Give the query a suitable name.

6 Click .

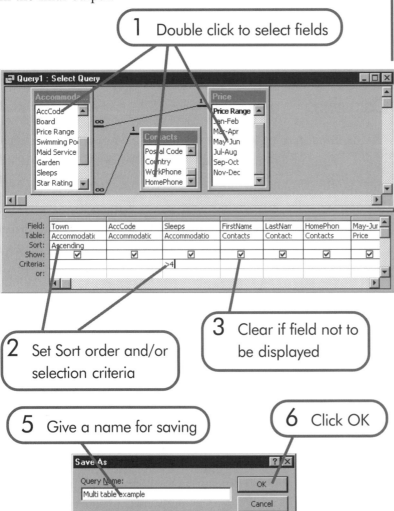

1 Double click to select fields

2 Set Sort order and/or selection criteria

3 Clear if field not to be displayed

5 Give a name for saving

6 Click OK

Take note

The query can be found in the Queries area of the Database window.

7 Click the Run tool 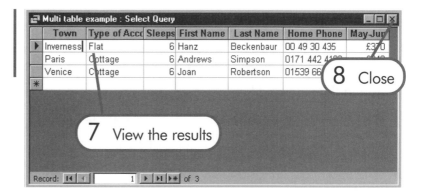 to see the results.

8 Close the query.

⑧ Close

⑦ View the results

Query listed in Database window

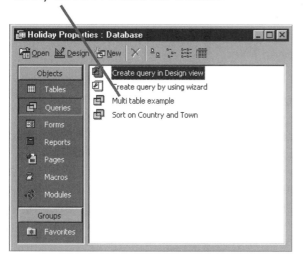

Relational operators

When setting criteria you can use relational operators:

>	more than	<	less than
=	equal to	<>	not equal to
>=	more than or equal to	<=	less than or equal to

These are mainly used for Number or Date/Time fields, but can be used with Text fields. > "H" means after H in the alphabet.

Summary

❑ If you are trying to locate specific data you can use the Find command.

❑ You can replace data in your table from the Replace tab in the Find and Replace dialog box.

❑ To obtain a subset of the records in your table you can either Filter By Selection or Filter By Form.

❑ The subdatasheet of a table can easily be expanded and collapsed to display and hide related records.

❑ Records can be sorted into ascending or descending order.

❑ Multi-level sorts must be set up in the Advanced Filter/ Sort dialog box, or as a query.

❑ Save your query if you wish to reuse it.

❑ You can use the Simple Query Wizard to combine fields from different tables/queries into one datasheet.

❑ To interrogate several tables at the same time, you must set up a query.

❑ Query criteria are entered into the Select Query grid.

❑ Relational operators are used to filter out the records required.

❑ To reuse a query, select it and click ▦ Open .

❑ To edit the criteria in a query that has been saved and closed, select the query in the Database window and click ▦ Design .

9 Forms

Designing a form

Forms allow you to customise your screen for input and editing purposes. Forms are particularly useful where the database is to be updated by other people as they allow simpler and more accurate data entry. We saw a basic form generated by Autoform in Chapter 6. Here, we will design from scratch a simple form to display the name, telephone number and address for our contacts.

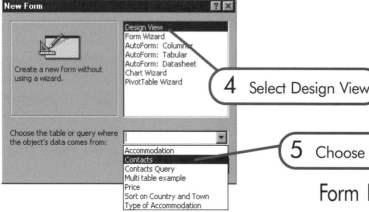

Basic steps

1   Select Forms in the Objects bar.

2   Double-click Create form in Design View.

or

3   Click [🗐 New] on the Database window toolbar.

4   Select Design View at the New Form dialog box.

5   Drop down the list of tables and queries and choose the table or query (*Contacts* in our case) that supplies data for the form.

6   Click [OK].

❑   You arrive at the Form Design screen.

Form Design toolbar

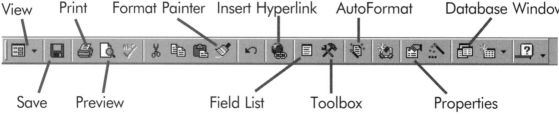

Basic steps

1 Right-click on the area outside the grid.

2 Select Properties from the Shortcut menu.

3 In the Form properties dialog box select the Data tab.

4 In the Record Source field, drop down the list and select your data source.

5 Close the Form properties dialog box.

Take note

Controls are objects that can be placed on a form, report or data access page. They can display data, perform actions or add decorative effects, e.g. lines or boxes.

Data source

The data source is the table or query that holds the data that is displayed in your form. When you create a new form by clicking 📋 New , you can identify your data source in the **New Form** dialog box.

However, if you double-click **Create form in Design View**, you arrive at the design grid without specifying the data source. You can identify, or change the data source from the design grid of your form.

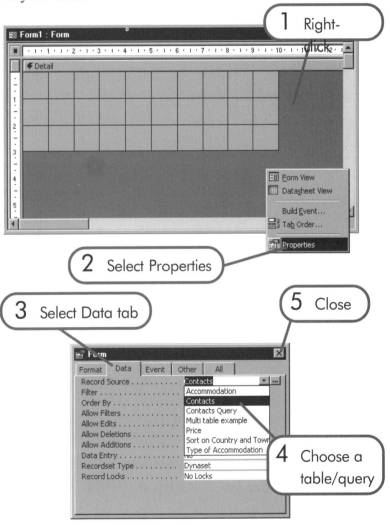

1 Right-click

2 Select Properties

3 Select Data tab

5 Close

4 Choose a table/query

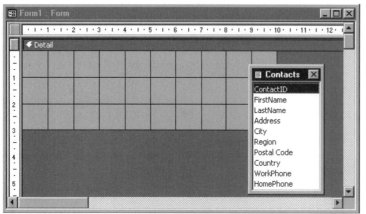

Field list displayed

The Toolbox

The Toolbox is used to add different controls to your from in Design View. Click the Toolbox tool on the Form Design toolbar to show or hide the Toolbox as necessary.

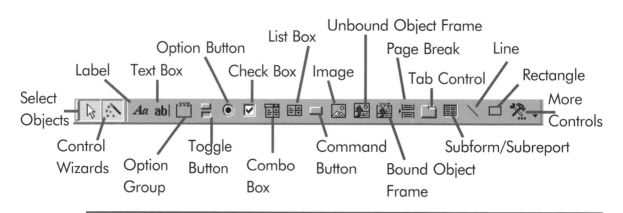

Header and footer

Basic steps

1 Open the View menu.

2 Choose Form Header/ Footer.

❑ A Form Header area appears above, and a Form Footer area appears below, the Detail area.

3 Resize the Form Header and Form Footer area as necessary by dragging the lower edge of the area, up or down (we need to increase the size of the Form Header and decrease the size of the Form Footer – in fact make it disappear!)

Usually, you will have some descriptive text in your form. This may be a heading for the whole form, column headings, or simply some narrative with instructions to the user.

In this example we want the form title and some descriptive text. This text, which we will put in the Form Header area, is called a **label**.

We must display the **Form Header** and **Footer** areas first, then insert the labels.

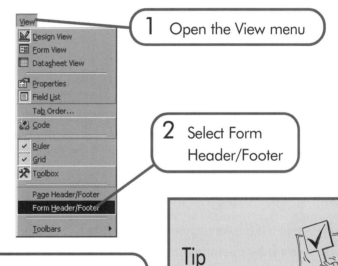

1 Open the View menu

2 Select Form Header/Footer

3 Resize as necessary

Tip

Check that the Snap to Grid option in the Format menu is on. This automatically aligns objects with points on the grid, making it easier to place labels and fields accurately during the design stage. When it is switched off, you can place objects anywhere.

Adding labels

The headings we are going to put on our form are purely descriptive – they are not part of the table the form is designed around. We can therefore make the text anything we want. This can be very useful for instructions.

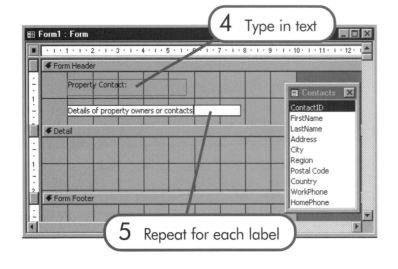

4 Type in text

5 Repeat for each label

1 Click the Label tool **Aa**.

2 Move the mouse pointer – now **⁺A** – to where you want your first label.

3 Click and drag to draw a rectangle.

4 Type in your label text e.g. *Property Contacts*.

5 Repeat steps 1–4 for the next label, e.g. *Details of property owners or contacts*.

Adjusting controls

If you position a label (or any control) incorrectly, or make it too big or small, you can easily fix it. First select it by clicking anywhere on it. Note the handles that appear around the edges of the selected control.

❑ To Resize

1 Point to a handle. The pointer changes to a double-headed arrow.

2 Drag the arrow to resize.

❑ To Move

1 Point to an edge (not a handle). The pointer changes to a hand.

2 Drag the element into position.

❑ To Delete

1 Press the [Delete] key.

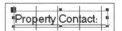

116

Basic steps

1 Select the label you want to format.

2 To change the font, drop down the list of fonts on the Formatting toolbar, and select from there.

3 To change the size of font, choose from the drop-down size list.

4 Toggle bold or *italics* to switch the format on or off.

Formatting the labels

Now that your labels are on your form, in the correct position and the correct size, you might want to enhance the appearance of them so they stand out clearly on your form. You might want to make them bigger, or bolder, or in italics – you choose!

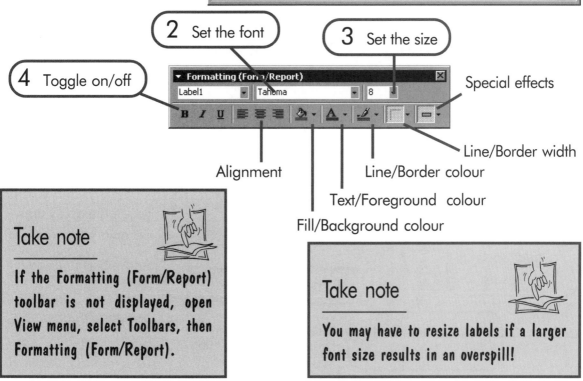

Take note

If the Formatting (Form/Report) toolbar is not displayed, open View menu, select Toolbars, then Formatting (Form/Report).

Take note

You may have to resize labels if a larger font size results in an overspill!

Adding fields

We now need to position the fields we require in the Detail area of the form. Clicking and dragging the required field from the field list to its destination on the form does this. When a field is dragged over however, it has two components – one for the field name and one for the field detail.

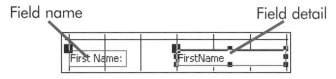

Field name   Field detail

First Name: FirstName

You can leave both parts on your form – or you could delete the field name part (as in this example) and use a label to describe the data.

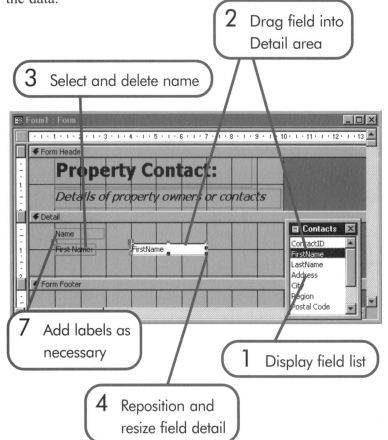

2 Drag field into Detail area

3 Select and delete name

Property Contact:

Details of property owners or contacts

Name

First Name: FirstName

Contacts

ContactID
FirstName
LastName
Address
City
Region
Postal Code

7 Add labels as necessary

1 Display field list

4 Reposition and resize field detail

1 Click the Field List tool ▤ to display the Field List (if it isn't visible).

2 Drag a field from the list (*FirstName*), and drop it in the Detail area.

❑ Both parts of the field are selected, but we want to deal with them separately.

3 Click on the field name section to select it, and press [Delete].

4 If necessary, reposition and/or resize the field detail component.

5 Repeat steps 2–4 for each field (*LastName, HomePhone, Work-Phone, Address,* etc.) as required.

6 Resize the detail area if necessary.

7 Add labels to explain data as necessary.

❑ See page 120 for the final layout.

Basic steps

Save your form

1   Use File – Save or click the Save tool ⬛ .

2   At the Save As dialog box, key in a name for your form.

3   Click [OK].

❑   The name will be appear in the Forms area in the Database window.

Obviously, you need to save your form design if you want to keep it. You can save at any time – you don't need to wait until you have set the whole thing up. If you are designing a complex form, save it regularly.

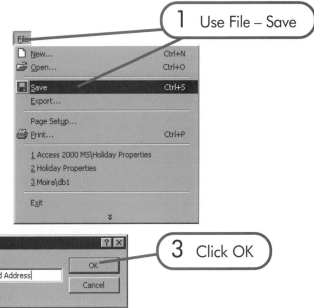

1   Use File – Save

File	
New...	Ctrl+N
Open...	Ctrl+O
Save	Ctrl+S
Export...	
Page Setup...	
Print...	Ctrl+P
1 Access 2000 MS\Holiday Properties	
2 Holiday Properties	
3 Moira\db1	
Exit	

2   Enter a name

Save As   ? X

Form Name:
Contact's Name, Phone and Address   [OK]
                                           [Cancel]

3   Click OK

Save and Save As

If you have already saved your form, and have edited the design since you last saved it, you can use **File – Save** to replace the old version of the form with the new one.

Save under a different name

Save As   ? X

Save Form 'Accommodation Simple Form' To: [OK]
Accommodation - not so simple form!   [Cancel]

As
Form   ▼

Object type

If you want to save the edited version as a separate form, use **File – Save As/Export...** to give a different name. This may be useful if you want to experiment with the design of an existing form, but without overwriting the original one.

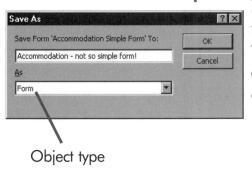

Form View

Let us look at our form in Form View, where one record will be displayed at a time on the screen.

It is assumed you are in the Form Design screen.

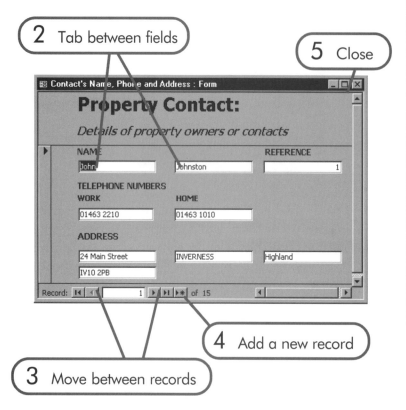

2 Tab between fields

5 Close

4 Add a new record

3 Move between records

1 Click the View tool or drop down the list and choose Form View.

❑ The form is displayed in Form View.

2 Use [Tab] to move from field to field.

3 Move from record to record using the forward and backward buttons.

4 Click the New Record button if you wish to add another record.

5 Close your form when you are finished.

Take note

If you are not happy with the look of the form when you see it in Form View, click the View tool to go back to Design View and edit it (remember to save any changes you make).

Take note

Data entered or edited on a form updates the table on which the form is based.

Basic steps

Form Design Wizard

1 Double click Create form by using Wizard at the Database window.

2 Work through the wizard, selecting the fields, layout, style, etc.

3 Click Finish at the final step, and the new form will be displayed.

You can also create forms quickly using the Form Design Wizard. Try it out – you may find it useful for some forms.

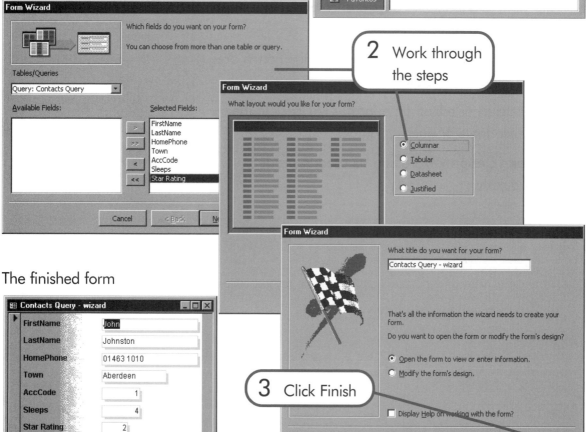

The finished form

121

Summary

❑ Forms allow you to customise your input and viewing screens.

❑ The Data Source is the table or query that contains the data displayed in the form.

❑ The Header and Footer areas can be used for headings, narrative or instructions you wish to display on your form.

❑ You can add fields anywhere on your form – simply drag the field from the field list onto the form grid.

❑ Text (for instructions and/or labels) can be included on your form to enhance its appearance and make it easier to use.

❑ If you save your form, it will be listed in the Forms area of the Database window.

❑ Data entered or edited on a form is fed back to the associated table or query.

❑ The Form Design Wizard can be used to produce forms quickly.

10 Reports

The Report Wizard

Reports provide the most effective way of creating a printed copy of data extracted or calculated from the tables and queries in your database. They might be invoices, purchase orders, mailing labels or materials to present information to customers or colleagues in a clear, unambiguous way.

Many of the features used in forms design are also used in report design. There are also a number of features that are unique to the report environment. You can build reports from scratch in much the same way as the form we created in the previous chapter – or you could try out some of the Report Wizards.

The example below uses a wizard to create a report that groups our properties by *Star Rating*, and lists details of the *Country*, *Town* and *Type of Accommodation* of each.

1   Select Reports in the Objects bar.

2   Click  .

3   At the New Report dialog box, select Report Wizard.

4   Choose the table on which you wish to base your report – *Accommodation* in our case.

5   Click ⬚ OK ⬚.

❑   You can control the size and appearance of everything in a report and can therefore display the information just as you want it.

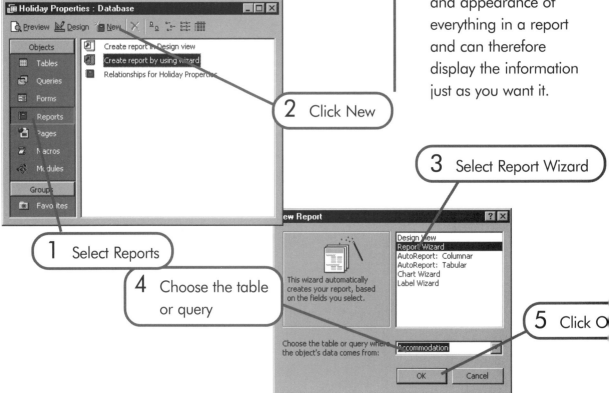

2   Click New

1   Select Reports

3   Select Report Wizard

4   Choose the table or query

5   Click O

Basic steps

1 Select the fields required for your report.

❏ You can select fields from more than one table if you wish.

2 Specify the *Star Rating* field as the grouping option.

❏ We want to group all our properties with Star Rating 1, all properties with Star Rating 2, etc.

cont...

Specifying the detail

The first stages of the Wizard are concerned with the details to be drawn from your database. The later ones specify the appearance of the report.

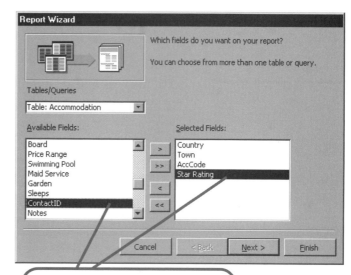

1 Select the fields to include

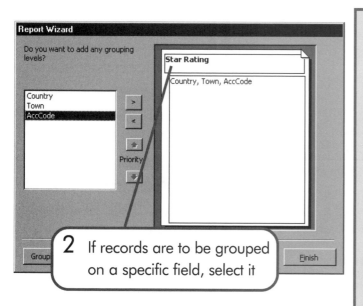

2 If records are to be grouped on a specific field, select it

Take note

To add grouping levels, select the field you wish to group on in the list on the the left and click ▶.

To remove a grouping level, select the field in the preview on the right and click ◀.

To move grouping levels relative to each other, select the field you wish to move in the preview and click ▲ or ▼ to move it up or down.

125

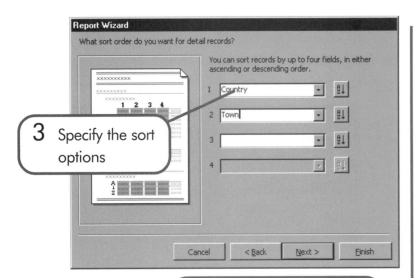

3 Specify the sort options

...cont

3 Set the sort options required.

4 Choose your report layout options.

5 Select the style you think most appropriate.

6 At the chequered flag, edit the name of your report if you wish.

7 Select Preview the report.

8 Click Finish.

4 Specify the layout options

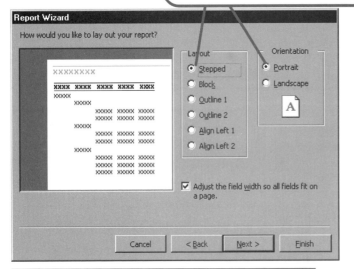

Take note

You can create a simple report using AutoReport in the New Object list. Select the table or query you wish to create an Autoreport from in the Database window, then select AutoReport from the New Object list. You can take the report into Design View to add headings, page numbering or the current date.

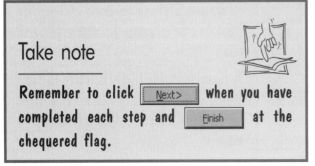

Take note

Remember to click Next> when you have completed each step and Finish at the chequered flag.

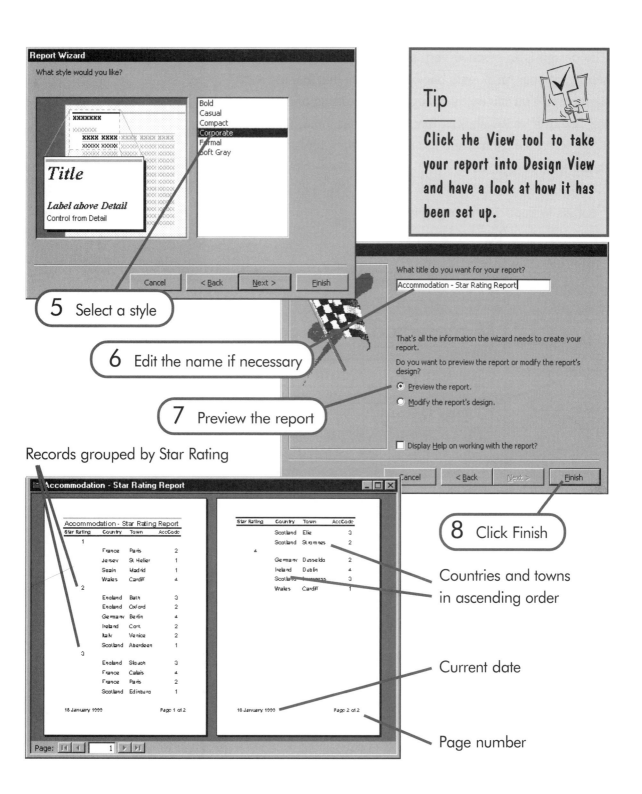

Report Wizard

What style would you like?

Title

Label above Detail
Control from Detail

Bold
Casual
Compact
Corporate
Formal
Soft Gray

Cancel   < Back   Next >   Finish

5   Select a style

Click the View tool to take your report into Design View and have a look at how it has been set up.

Tip

6   Edit the name if necessary

7   Preview the report

What title do you want for your report?

Accommodation - Star Rating Report

That's all the information the wizard needs to create your report.

Do you want to preview the report or modify the report's design?

● Preview the report.

○ Modify the report's design.

☐ Display Help on working with the report?

Cancel   < Back   Next >   Finish

Records grouped by Star Rating

Accommodation - Star Rating Report

Accommodation - Star Rating Report

Star Rating	Country	Town	AccCode
1			
	France	Paris	2
	Jersey	St. Helier	1
	Spain	Madrid	1
	Wales	Cardiff	4
2			
	England	Bath	3
	England	Oxford	2
	Germany	Berlin	4
	Ireland	Cork	2
	Italy	Venice	2
	Scotland	Aberdeen	1
3			
	England	Slough	3
	France	Calais	4
	France	Paris	2
	Scotland	Edinburg	1

18 January 1999   Page 1 of 2

Star Rating	Country	Town	AccCode
	Scotland	Elie	3
	Scotland	Stromness	2
4			
	Germany	Dusseldo	2
	Ireland	Dublin	4
	Scotland	Inverness	3
	Wales	Cardiff	1

18 January 1999   Page 2 of 2

Page: 1

8   Click Finish

Countries and towns in ascending order

Current date

Page number

The design

The design is in essence very similar to what you did when setting up your form, with one or two extra bits that are useful on reports. You can easily change the formatting of any part of the design if you wish – its font size, colour, bold, italics, etc. – just select the control and use the formatting tools as you did in the form design window.

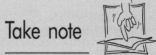

Take note

The Sorting and Grouping tool is a toggle – you can use it to open and close the Sorting and Grouping dialog box.

Labels in Report and Page Header

Group Header

Current date code in Text Box

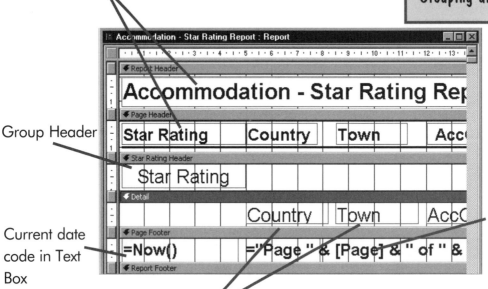

Page number code in Text Box

Fields from *Accommodation* table

- The Report Header and Page Header contain Labels that have been formatted.

- The Report Header/Footer and Page Header/Footer areas can be switched on and off through the View menu.

Take note

To format several controls in the same way, select the first, then hold down [Shift] and select the rest – then format them all.

Expressions

Page numbers and dates, and other data, can be added to reports by using an expression, entered into a Text Box.

An expression is a combinatio of text, symbols and special functions, e.g.:

=Now() displays the current date

=[Page] displays the page number

= "Page " & [Page] displays 'Page' followed by the page number

The Report Wizard automatically puts two expressions in the Page Footer of the report.

● The *Star Rating* Header is a Group Header. Click the Sorting and Grouping tool to see how this has been set up.

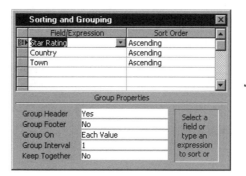

● The Detail area contains fields from the *Accommodation* table.

● The Page Footer contains expressions that return the current date *=Now()* and the page numbering format = *"Page " & [Page] "of " & [Pages]* for the report. The expressions are entered into Text Boxes, created using the Text Box tool ab|.

● Drawing tools have been used to draw lines and borders around areas of the report. Click the line or rectangle drawing tool, then click and drag on your report to draw the shape. To change the colour or width of the line or border, select it then use the Line/Border Color tool, or Line/Border Width tool to get the effect you want.

Line tool   Rectangle tool

Line/Border Color   Line/Border Width

AutoFormat

You can easily apply or change formatting using an AutoFormat – a set of predefined formatting options – in a report or form. You can save your own formatting options as an AutoFormat, so that you can apply them to other forms or reports in the future.

1. Display the report or form in Design View.

2. Click the Autoformat tool.

3. Select another style from the list if required.

4. Click `Options >>` if you wish to adjust the attributes.

5. Select or deselect the attributes as required.

❑ To save your formatting into a new layout

6. Click Customize...

7. Select the top option and click `OK`.

8. Enter a name for your new style.

9. Click `OK`.

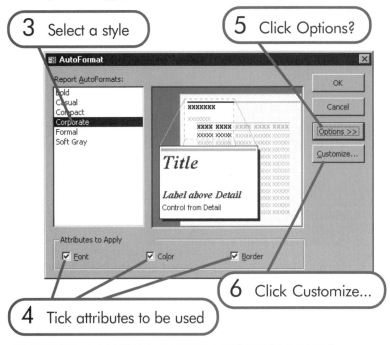

3 Select a style

5 Click Options?

4 Tick attributes to be used

6 Click Customize...

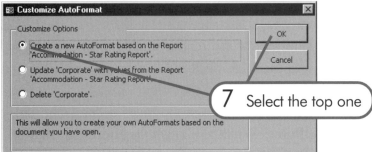

7 Select the top one

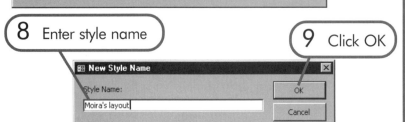

8 Enter style name

9 Click OK

Take note

If you try to update or delete the built-in styles, a prompt will tell you that it is not allowed!!

130

Basic steps

1 In the Report Design window, click the Print Preview tool , or select a preview option from the View drop-down list.

2 If the preview looks okay, click the Print tool to print your report.

3 Close the Print Preview window.

Preview and print

You can Print Preview your report, and print out a hard copy if you wish. There are two Preview choices here. The **Layout Preview** will give you a quick preview using some of your data. The **Print Preview** takes longer to produce, but gives you a preview of all of the data that will appear in your report.

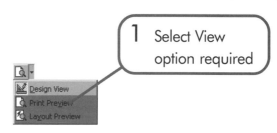

1 Select View option required

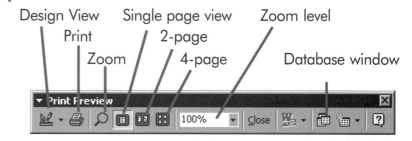

Design View
Print
Zoom
Single page view
2-page
4-page
Zoom level
Database window

Take note

You can print directly from the Print Design screen, without first doing a preview. Click the Print tool on the Report Design toolbar.

Tip

If you've made changes to the report design, don't forget to save if you want to keep the changes. Click to save.

Take note

If you close the Preview window using the Close tool on the toolbar, you are returned to the Report Design screen. If you close the Preview window by single-clicking the Close button ⊠, you are returned to the Database window.

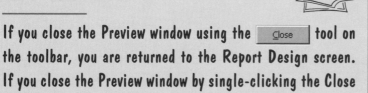

131

Summary

❏ Reports provide an effective way of presenting data extracted or calculated from your queries and tables.

❏ Many of the techniques used in Form design are also used in Report design, e.g. placing fields, adding descriptive text, formatting.

❏ Wizards can speed up the Report design stage.

❏ The designs generated by a Wizard can be customised to suit your exact requirements.

❏ Expressions to display the current date or a page number can be entered into Text Boxes

❏ The Drawing tools can be used to add emphasis to your reports.

❏ You can apply, edit, save or delete AutoFormats from Design View in reports or forms.

❏ It is a good idea to preview your report before you print – you can then check the layout of your report before you commit it to paper.

11 Database Wizard

Selecting a Wizard

In addition to creating a database from scratch, as we have done in this book, you could use a Database Wizard to help you set up your tables, forms and reports.

There are several ready-made databases that you can modify easily using a Wizard. Have a look through them to see if any could be useful to you.

Basic steps

1 Click the New tool.

2 Select the Databases tab.

3 Pick a database.

4 Click OK.

5 Create and name your database as shown on page 24.

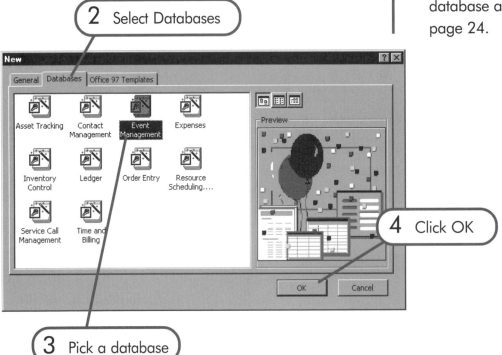

2 Select Databases

3 Pick a database

4 Click OK

Take note

The databases have full sets of fields and predesigned forms and reports. The Wizard simply helps you modify them.

Basic steps

1 Click [Next>] at the introductory panel.

2 Choose a table.

3 Select or deselect the fields as required.

4 Repeat steps 2 and 3 for all the tables.

The first thing you need to do is customise the tables in your database. You do this by specifying the fields you want to include or leave out of each table.

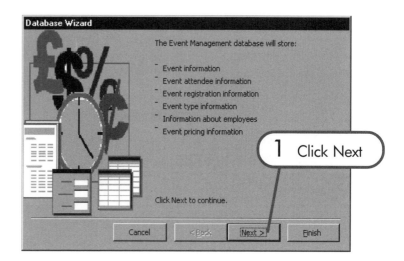

1 Click Next

2 Select a table

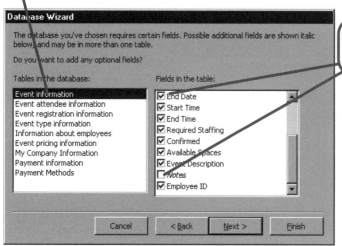

3 Select/deselect the fields for the table

4 Repeat for other tables

Take note

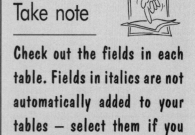

Check out the fields in each table. Fields in italics are not automatically added to your tables — select them if you wish to include them.

Setting the style

The next steps in the Wizard let you select options that control the screen display and the printed reports. There are several options to choose from – browse through them until you find something you like.

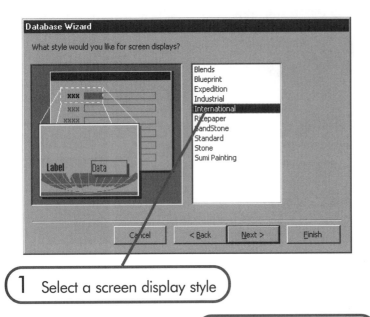

1 Select a screen display style

2 Select a report style

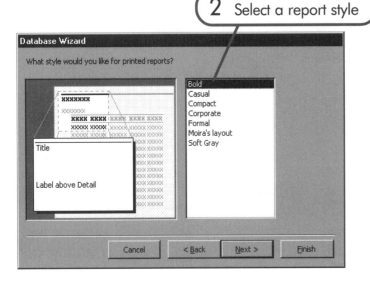

Basic steps

1 Select a style for the screen display.

2 Choose a style for your printed reports.

3 Give your database a title.

4 Select the Yes, I'd like to include a picture box if you want a picture on each report.

5 Click **Picture...** and select the picture from your disk.

6 If you want to start work on the database straight away, select Yes, start the database at the final step.

7 Click **Finish** then wait while the Wizard completes your database.

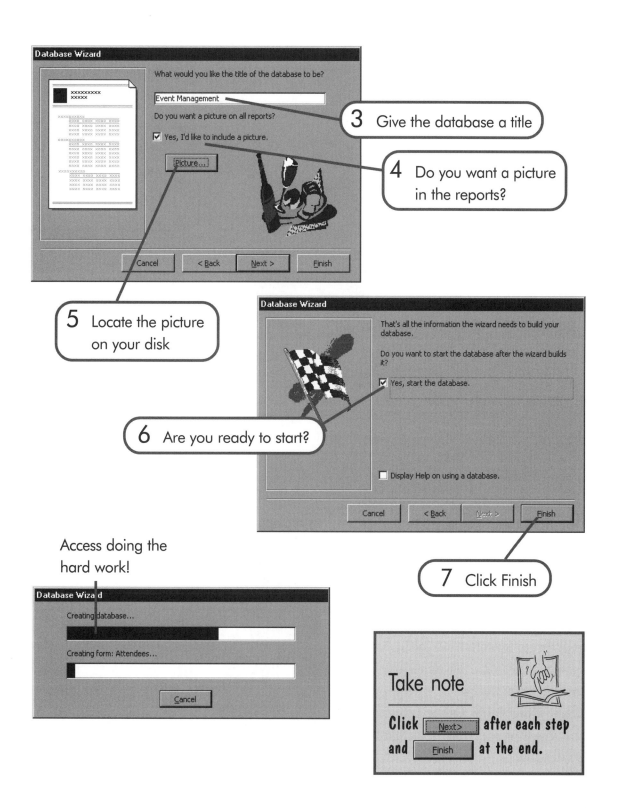

Database Wizard

What would you like the title of the database to be?

Event Management

Do you want a picture on all reports?

☑ Yes, I'd like to include a picture.

Picture...

Cancel | < Back | Next > | Finish

3 Give the database a title

4 Do you want a picture in the reports?

5 Locate the picture on your disk

Database Wizard

That's all the information the wizard needs to build your database.

Do you want to start the database after the wizard builds it?

☑ Yes, start the database.

☐ Display Help on using a database.

Cancel | < Back | Next > | Finish

6 Are you ready to start?

7 Click Finish

Access doing the hard work!

Database Wizard

Creating database...

Creating form: Attendees...

Cancel

Take note

Click [Next>] after each step and [Finish] at the end.

137

The end product

Company information

Some databases will use your company name and address on forms and reports. You will be prompted to enter this information before you start to use the database.

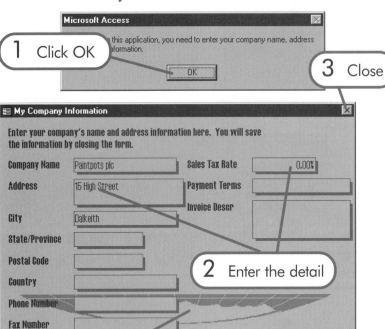

1 Click OK

3 Close

2 Enter the detail

Picture included

Take note

As with those that you design yourself, you can take any form or report into Design View (except the Switchboard) and modify them if you wish.

The Main Switchboard

The Switchboard

This acts as a 'front end' to your database, giving easy access to your forms and reports. Switchboards are like a menu system. The Main Switchboard is the starting point and some of the options here – **Enter/View Other Information** and **Preview Reports** – lead to other Switchboards.

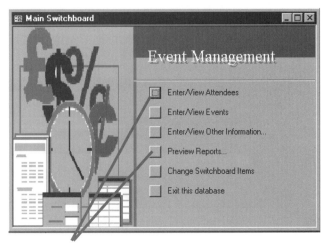

Click to display forms and reports

Explore the forms and
reports in your database

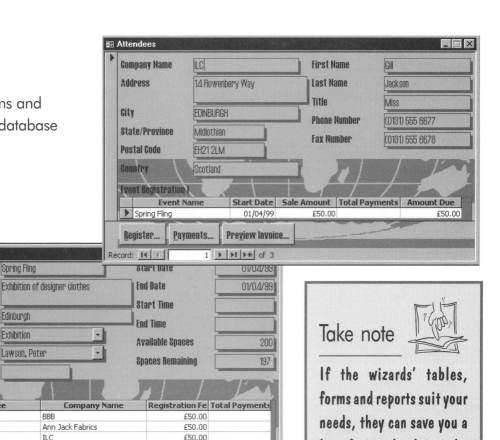

Take note

If the wizards' tables,
forms and reports suit your
needs, they can save you a
lot of time by doing the
ground work.

Take note

To display the database window, click ☒
on the Main Switchboard title bar, then
restore the database window, which is
minimised at the bottom left of the
screen. To reopen the Main Switchboard,
double-click on the Switchboard form in
the Database window.

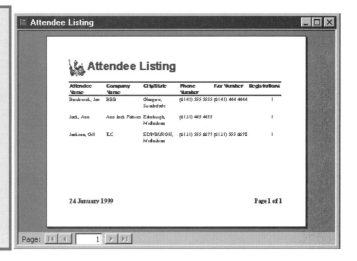

Summary

❑ There are several Database Wizards for you to choose from.

❑ You can customise your tables by selecting or deselecting the fields for each table.

❑ There are several screen display and report options to choose from to set the style for your database.

❑ Switchboards provide a user-friendly 'front end' to your forms and reports.

Appendix

Type of Accommodation

AccCode	Description
1	Apartment
2	Cottage
3	Flat
4	Room

Price

Price Range	Jan-Feb	Mar-Apr	May-Jun	Jul-Aug	Sep-Oct	Nov-Dec
A	£240	£260	£300	£350	£310	£260
B	£260	£280	£320	£380	£320	£280
C	£275	£296	£340	£390	£360	£300
D	£285	£310	£370	£420	£390	£350
E	£300	£340	£410	£470	£425	£395

Take note

If you don't want to type in this data, the tables can be downloaded from:

http://www.madesimple.co.uk

Accommodation

Ref	Season Start	Season End	Type of Accomm	Town	Country	Board	Swim Pool	Maid Serv.	Garden	Price Range	Sleeps	Star Rating	Contact ID
1			A	Aberdeen	Scotland	HB	No	No	Yes	B	4	2	1
2			F	Slough	England	SC	No	Yes	No	C	4	3	2
3	01/02/99	01/12/99	R	Cardiff	Wales	BB	No	Yes	No	B	2	1	3
4			C	Cork	Ireland	SC	No	Yes	Yes	B	4	2	4
5	18/01/99	10/12/99	F	Inverness	Scotland	SC	Yes	Yes	No	D	6	4	5
6			C	Paris	France	SC	No	Yes	Yes	A	4	3	6
7			R	Berlin	Germany	HB	No	Yes	Yes	A	2	2	7
8			C	Dusseldorf	Germany	SC	No	Yes	Yes	B	4	4	7
9			C	Paris	France	SC	No	Yes	Yes	C	6	1	6
10			A	Edinburgh	Scotland	HB	Yes	Yes	No	D	4	3	8
11			F	Bath	England	SC	Yes	Yes	No	D	4	2	9
12			A	Cardiff	Wales	BB	Yes	No	Yes	E	4	4	3
13			F	Elie	Scotland	SC	No	Yes	No	E	4	3	1
14			C	Venice	Italy	SC	Yes	Yes	Yes	C	6	2	10
15			A	Madrid	Spain	SC	Yes	Yes	No	D	4	1	11
16			C	Oxford	England	SC	No	Yes	Yes	C	4	2	2
17			R	Calais	France	BB	No	Yes	Yes	C	2	3	12
18			C	Stromness	Orkney	SC	No	Yes	Yes	B	4	3	1
19			A	St. Helier	Jersey	SC	Yes	Yes	Yes	C	4	1	13
20			R	Dublin	Ireland	HB	Yes	Yes	Yes	D	2	4	14

Contacts

ContactID	FirstName	LastName	Address	City	County	Post Code	Country	Work Phone	Home Phone
1	John	Johnston	24 Main Street	INVERNESS	Highland	IV10 2PB	Scotland	01463 2210	01463 1010
2	Elaine	Anderson	22 St Stephen Street	EDINBURGH	Midlothian	EH10 3PR	Scotland	0131 442 1021	0131 556 0212
3	Elizabeth	Watson	14 Mill Wynd West	GLASGOW	Strathclyde	G13 3AB	Scotland	0141 665 1043	0141 510 5103
4	Gordon	McPherson	14 Worthington Way	BIRMINGHAM	Midlands	B24 2DS	England	0121 557 9321	0121 676 1999
5	Hanz	Beckenbaur	24 Lang Strasse	BERLIN			Germany	00 49 30 121	00 49 30 435
6	Andrew	Simpson	10 Dolphin Road	LONDON		N18 2WS	England	0181 475 1010	0171 442 4102
7	Alice	Aberley	St Stephens Manse	PETERLEE	Co Durham	SR8 5AJ	England	0191 575 3928	0191 653 1843
8	Brian	Allanson	328 Bath Road	ILFORD	Essex	IG2 6PN	England	0181 543 6758	0171 544 1234
9	Pamela	Johnston	10 Wilson Way	DEREHAM	Norfolk	NR19 1JG	England	01362 331112	01362 574098
10	Joan	Robertson	24 West Linton Way	KENDAL	Cumbria	LA9 6EH	England	01539 561732	01539 665577
11	William	Flux	132 London Road	CARNO	Montgomery	SY17 5LU	Wales	01686 203956	01686 105619
12	Amanda	Wilson	14 High Way	LAMPETER	Dyfed	SA4 8NW	Wales	01570 30651	01570 61234
13	William	Robertson	Hill View Rise	STROMNESS	Orkney	OK10 3AB	Scotland	01856 103212	01856 114322
14	Suzanne	Young	24 Causeway St	CLEMENT	Jersey	J21 2ED	Channel Is	01534 14261	01534 66310
15	Paul	Mitchell	45 Hill Top View	ABERDEEN	Aberdeenshire	AB24	Scotland	01224 10231	01224 54123

Index